MAIN
STREET
SMARTS

MAIN STREET SMARTS

DAVID
MORGAN

SUCCESS AT THE
INTERSECTION OF

MAIN STREET

AND

WALL STREET

Advantage®

Published by Advantage, Charleston, South Carolina.
Member of Advantage Media Group.

ADVANTAGE is a registered trademark and the Advantage colophon is a trademark of Advantage Media Group, Inc.

Printed in the United States of America.

ISBN: 978-1-59932-628-3
LCCN: 2016948939

Cover design by George Stevens.

This publication is designed to provide accurate and authoritative information in regard to the subject matter covered. It is sold with the understanding that the publisher is not engaged in rendering legal, accounting, or other professional services. If legal advice or other expert assistance is required, the services of a competent professional person should be sought.

Advantage Media Group is proud to be a part of the Tree Neutral® program. Tree Neutral offsets the number of trees consumed in the production and printing of this book by taking proactive steps such as planting trees in direct proportion to the number of trees used to print books. To learn more about Tree Neutral, please visit **www.treeneutral.com.** To learn more about Advantage's commitment to being a responsible steward of the environment, please visit **www.advantagefamily.com/green**

Advantage Media Group is a publisher of business, self-improvement, and professional development books and online learning. We help entrepreneurs, business leaders, and professionals share their Stories, Passion, and Knowledge to help others Learn & Grow. Do you have a manuscript or book idea that you would like us to consider for publishing? Please visit **advantagefamily.com** or call **1.866.775.1696.**

This book would not be possible without all the people I've had the good fortune to stand with, side by side, facing the greatest challenges and taking on the tremendous adventure of "business."

TABLE OF CONTENTS

ACKNOWLEDGMENTS

First and foremost I have to acknowledge my father, Ted, and brother, Doug, with whom I have worked for almost all of my adult life. Although this book is written from my point of view, it might not have been possible to achieve without what we have done together. There were longer nights and more stressful days than I can remember. Without each of us pulling the load at times, the road may never have ever gotten to where we are today.

From STS, Charlie, Vicky, and Vicki, who have been with us almost since the beginning. They believed and stuck through with us even when times were the toughest. Their loyalty, dedication, and perseverance will always be remembered.

From my time at business school, my MBA classmates at the University of Maryland, who taught me more about myself than I could have ever learned in a book. I have the utmost respect for Andrew Sherman, who developed from a professor to a friend. The energy he brings and his ability to cut through the crap and deliver the messages you need to hear are priceless.

My friend, Tim Day, who faced every challenge in his life with passion and commitment. With each of us growing businesses over the last twenty years, we always had a safe harbor where we could share stories, complain, laugh, and celebrate the courage it takes, and at times the incredible sacrifice necessary, to actually pursue your dreams. It was during one of those very late nights at some bar, telling stories, that we came up with the idea for this book.

My brother Dan, sister Jenny, and mom Patti. They have all been part of this journey at times and in their own ways. They have each taught me to have the personal confidence to commit to your decisions, persevere toward your goals, and fight for your dreams.

Finally, my wife, Amy, who has shown nothing but unwavering support and patience for everything that I have tried to do.

I am a successful businessman who went to a traditional business school. In fact, I have even lectured at business schools. But I am here to tell you that most of what I learned about running a profitable, successful business I did *not* learn in business school. And here's why.

Too often, most of what you are taught in business school either centers on very analytical frameworks developed to evaluate marketing strategies or focuses on financials. The process is theoretical and academic, analyzing the past to predict the future or learning from case studies to apply the past to the present. Business schools produce a lot of hype about prestigous companies like Facebook, Google, IBM, and Black & Decker. They also tend to focus on a certain person as if that one person created all the success. But here's the secret they don't tell you: the man behind the curtain, "The Wizard of Oz" if you will, is a fallacy. He's far removed from the actual worker that produces value. These icons of industry do not stem from small businesses, which are the fundamental part of the economy. I've been fortunate to work with very senior leaders in the federal government, in the Department of Defense, and in industry, and I can honestly say that I would not necessarily hire any of them to work at my business despite their success and standing. Why not? Because they simply don't understand what it takes to run a small business and make it work every day. They lack the street skills it takes to drive a small business. This is not to say these are not good people, successful in their own environments—environments with a lot of cash, market access, and infrastructure that they did not bring to the table themselves. What I am saying is that the skills from that environment do not automatically translate into the ability to create, develop, and grow a business.

Most masters of business administration (MBA) programs are simply not tailored for small business. Some exist as a large profit center for universities because they receive a tremendous amount of institutional support from industries that will pay for students to take classes. MBA programs can generate money for the rest of the university. Since they can be such a large revenue source, there is a need to craft their "sell." So their calling card tends toward, "Attend our program and you can be the next CEO or create the next Google or Facebook"—as I said, a somewhat false ad.

Business schools also promote their MBA programs as the key to opening up doors and providing students with the access to become a high-level manager. Again, this can be a myth. Just because you have an MBA and can read a cash flow statement or interpret a balance sheet does not necessarily make you ready to be a CEO or business owner.

It's in all the soft skills where most MBA programs fail. For instance, they don't teach you the decision-making skills you need, so you end up lacking the architecture on how to make a confident decision. They don't teach you how to build an effective team. But the main area they come up short on, a concept they don't even approach, is they don't teach you how to sell.

Most MBA programs will elevate you by teaching you the art of management or how to be a good leader but fail you by not talking about selling. How does that hurt you? The reality is that everything about owning a business, everything about business itself, is about *selling*. It's about selling yourself every day that you walk into the office. It's about selling your idea, selling it to your team, selling it to your boss, selling it to your customer. Most business school programs don't like to discuss that part of business, which is actually the part that produces the most revenue for a company.

What business schools focus on instead is selling the dream of becoming the CEO. What they fail to instill in their students is that to become the CEO, you have to be able to sell. In order to become successful you have to be able to sell your idea to everyone, and the reality is that just because you're a good leader doesn't necessarily mean you're a good seller.

This is not to say that you don't need to be able to read the balance sheets and do the analytics to run a business. Those are very valid skills. But the core of what business schools need to teach you often isn't taught, and that is the art of hustle. Are you willing to get up earlier in the morning to be the first one into the office? Are you willing to make the phone calls, to set up the appointments, to rush around to get to a potential client, to dig deep to secure revenue, to take risks that no one else will own? At the end of the day it's all about the execution. I can take a bad idea with a great team and make it more successful than working a great idea with a bad team.

Don't misunderstand. MBA programs can be a good tool and framework for building relationships with your peers. They can teach you some advanced skills. You will learn to communicate in a professional manner with other people. But you can also learn those skills at the office by paying attention. If you're going to get your MBA, don't kid yourself into thinking that those three letters after your name alone are going to secure your career goal. They will likely facilitate the advantage of getting your foot in the door. But truly securing your career goal will only happen based on your own hard work.

When I started my business career, it was pure happenstance. I was on track to go to medical school and realized it wasn't for me. At the time, my dad was starting a business and asked me if I'd like to be one of the cofounders. I said "sure," with no understanding of what I was getting into. As the company's success grew, I took the opportunity to get my MBA. I learned a lot about myself in those twenty-four months. And I learned a lot about analytics. But I also learned a lot of three-syllable words for the two-syllable words I had learned on the street. What business school didn't teach me were the fundamentals that come with starting and creating a business: the tremendous hours it takes, the financial risk that comes with it, the loss of holidays and vacations and weekends, the gambling of what money you have, or the risk of borrowing against your house. What they couldn't give me experience in was how to take a business and grow it, how to make the hard decisions and put them into an appropriate framework, or how to develop the confidence and maturity to run a business. What I learned was that most MBA programs are not tailored for small businesses, and yet small businesses create 70 percent of jobs in this country. This means most of their graduates *will* end up working in the small business sphere.

The small business world is a Wild West environment to be working in, where you will constantly fight to validate your concept. Take for example the early years of our company, STS International. Every day was a new adventure—walking out, trying to figure out how to make the company successful and how to do it on a dime. My dad had emptied out his bank account and gambled everything on the company. We were challenged not only to sell the concept but also to produce the goods, and we were learning on the fly. Sometimes we were successful, other times we made a decision and then realized it was a dumb idea and that we had just spent a lot of money to build a feature that didn't work. It was hard work, it was challenging, and it was scary at times, but it was also fun and exciting.

In this book, I want to share with you some practical lessons and experiences from my own path. I want to reveal the mistakes I've made from which I have benefited in the long run. I can show you how to craft a business plan that will help you start your new business or grow your existing business. Most of all, I can teach you how to *sell yourself.*

ONE

LESSONS FROM THE FRONT

(STREET SMARTS 101)

There are lessons you learn in business school, and then there are lessons you learn on the street. The story of self-made success and the underdog is an iconic one in this country. During my time in business with my father and brother, starting with little more than an idea and almost no money, we grew a business that has now serviced customers in over eighteen countries around the world.

IN THE BEGINNING

My dad was that kind of businessman. He grew up in a very small town in rural Kentucky and enlisted in the army right after high school. From there, he attended military prep school and then went on to West Point. After two decades of service in the army, my dad retired and went to work for a secure communications company that sold point-to-point fax machines. He did that for a number of years and then decided to start his own business.

When my dad asked me to join the business, this changed our "father and son" relationship. Obviously he was still my father, but he was also my boss and business partner. Since he was technically my boss, whatever he said went. At the same time, I was his peer, since I was an owner and cofounder. Thus early on I had all these different facets and dynamics of our relationship that I was trying to manage.

My younger brother had just graduated from law school and opened his own law practice. He did that for a number of years while also doing all the legal work for our company. He finally changed course and joined my dad and me full time.

SOME LESSONS CAN'T BE TAUGHT, THEY MUST BE LEARNED

We started STS as a company with two main lines of business. One was a product that was a peripheral supporting device to secure telephones. Back in the 1990s the government used point-to-point phones that you could encrypt to have a conversation. My father saw an opportunity for a device that could help integrate the use of those phones.

The other line of our business was medical simulation. I had some experience with this concept from my premed and paramedic training, so my goal was to figure out how to use computers to generate medical simulation products to train people before they began practicing on humans. Prior to medical simulation, medical students would practice on an orange the first time they tried giving a shot. Then they would practice on their partner in the classroom. The next thing you know, they're giving real patients shots. So there was a real gap between sticking fruit with a needle and sticking a needle into a patient, and medical simulation filled that gap.

STS started with those two programs, and both became very successful. Then we discovered an opportunity to develop a biometrics program for the Department of Defense. Biometrics are physiological and/or behavioral characteristics that can be used to verify the identity of an individual person. At the time, fingerprinting was only done by the penal system and for FBI background checks. Today, there is considerable advanced research into different types of biometrics, such as using your iris (the colored part of your eyes), your voice, and your face. There's even vein pattern recognition. We had the chance to propose a program to the United States Army to help them create a program where all their biometric activity could be coordinated and cleared, and you wouldn't have to figure out how to use it to support military applications. With those three business lines, we went from twelve employees to seventy-five employees in less than two years.

We chased the American dream to build a successful company. And I learned a lot along the way. One of the biggest street lessons I learned from my father was the value of perseverance, which still is part of the company culture. My dad probably has the strongest will of any person I've ever met. Regardless of the challenges that are in front of him, no matter if they are financial, intellectual, business, or political, his ability to continue to fight, to advocate for a position, and to win is unmatched.

We have been very successful at adapting to new industries and new customer segments because of his perseverance. Success is *not* just tied to creativity. It can also become an issue of sticking with something long enough and being willing to sacrifice the hours in the office or the hours away from home on nights and weekends and holidays to make it work. We were well known for never saying no to a customer. We would always listen to what they wanted.

GREAT WORKS ARE PERFORMED NOT BY STRENGTH, BUT BY PERSEVERANCE

Two specific examples stand out regarding our perseverance. First was the creation of the company. At the beginning of the company's concept, there was a program called "The Portable Uninterruptible Power Supply" program (PUP). PUP was a secure communications peripheral device that allowed storage between multiple systems. That was my dad's vision, and he persevered through a significant amount of stress to create the concept. Then he came up with his own prototype and convinced the government to fund it.

The sheer magnitude of going from working in a basement office with some two-drawer filing cabinets and a used door for a desk, to ramping up to produce a product was enormous. Every day, we'd hit a roadblock or a dead end. For instance, we had to figure out how to make our own submersible tank. We needed to submerge these enclosures under three feet of saltwater to make sure they didn't leak. We did not have the funding to go to a formal test lab and pay thousands of dollars for a test. How did we create this? We literally used an old heating oil tank, the kind of tank you use to store heating oil to heat your house. We cut it open, cleaned it out, and fabricated a winch to lower it in and lock it in place under six feet of water. That's just one of countless examples where we had to create our own solutions. Another street lesson: where there is no solution, create one. That's the kind of perseverance my dad had.

Another street lesson I learned is loyalty. Loyalty goes a long way in building a company culture. You've got to trust your people and advocate for them. You need to make sure they understand that the decisions you are making are in their best interest and the best interest of the organization. When you ask them to do something, they have to believe in why you're asking it and believe that it is in their best interest and not out of some selfish motivation.

Here's an example that combined my dad's perseverance and loyalty: At one point, we had a program that was going to be the next big step for the company. It would really move the needle and put us on the map. But as our company grew, so did the attention on STS, and over time we ended up having to compete for our contracts. When the re-competes came up, more and more competitors started pushing us out, one by one. We started losing task orders that we had worked on for several years. Eventually we got to the point where the competition was so severe that we had lost our last task order. We had dozens of staff members and no work.

There was a big gap from when we lost the last task order to when we thought we were going to get funded on our next big project. Out of sheer loyalty and perseverance, we didn't lay a single person off. We knew it wasn't their fault that we had lost the contract or that this other contract had yet to materialize. Over what became an eight-month gap, we carried all our employees on the payroll—every single one of them. We were determined to make this right. We fought every single day as opposed to laying everyone off or shutting down the company. Fortunately we had a line of credit that covered us for a while, but that maxed out. We cut all of our expenses to focus only on critical needs for the business and even had to put in personal money to cover payroll. Was it the right decision? A lot of other companies wouldn't do that. I think it's a testament to the way the company is organized, the way the company is looked upon internally, and the way we look at staff. There have been conversations at times when it felt as if we were shoveling money into a furnace, watching it go out, saying, "We can lay all these people off or shut down this facility and save a bunch of money." We've had those conversations plenty of times. But we've never pulled the trigger. Which is not to say this couldn't happen in the future. It does become a financial challenge as you get bigger and bigger. It is one thing to say you've got five employees and you're not going to lay them off. It's a whole different thing when you have fifty or five hundred people and you don't lay them off. Fortunately, we haven't had to make that decision. Hopefully, we never will. Today we're still moving forward after twenty-plus years of business.

BIG THINKING PRECEDES GREAT ACHIEVEMENTS

Street smarts require a certain amount of "big-picture" thinking. Because of our abilities to see the larger picture, we've been years ahead of the curve on technologies and concepts that are now pervasive in the Department of Defense.

I'm not a big-picture guy. I'm more the kind of guy who says, "I can get across the river. Give me a chance, and I'll figure out how to do it." I will leap from one rock to the next, then the next and the next, and get to the other side of the river. It's a very different approach from the big vision view of the world. I may not be able to see everything clearly, but I can understand that there are targets out there that can be pursued. I'm the guy who can jump quickly to the next target and get to the end objective.

Understanding that I was not a big picture or visionary kind of guy, I learned to make decisions quickly and to see when we were not at a sustainable place. I could take that challenge and use it to propel us into a new line of business. That's how I have adapted the big-picture skills. I can take any opportunity and quickly process it in a framework and say, "This is a decision we need to make for the company. We're going to move on this one." Not all of the big ideas come to fruition. Timing is critical to make big things happen. But in order to make things happen, you have to have confidence in your beliefs. That comes from having the ability to comprehend the big picture and then to make the decision to move forward. While my dad is always looking way out there to see huge opportunities and at times even creating the big picture when others do not see it, I'm the guy who figures out where the opportunity is and how to drive through today to get there tomorrow and the day after.

Those are just some of the street lessons I've learned from experience, mistakes, and challenges. One of the most important lessons has been that failure is not only an option; sometimes it is an inevitable outcome of decisions that you make. In fact, sometimes quitting is the better, more difficult option, especially if you've been cultivating a big idea and have invested time, money, and soul into it. Something that you know is going to be damaging is not worth the injury you will sustain from it. Sometimes just saying, "You know what, I'm just walking away. This one is not a good option," is the right decision.

But of all the choices you make, the biggest regret you will ever have is not trying simply because you are scared. You've got to get on the field. If you don't ever try to get on the field and play with a team and compete, you're going to blink and the world is going to go by. You'll be sitting there twenty years later, thinking, *I wish I could have,* or, *I wish I had done it.*

Having the courage to try is difficult. To be able to persevere and have the confidence, the survival skills, and the instincts to decide to either continue down a path or to correct your course is the hardest thing. You have to try and never give up. You have to persevere, be loyal, and see the big picture. You have to have the courage to compete. There are a lot of analogies between sports and business. Some of it is true and other parts not so much. It is true that you, and your team, try to outperform the competition based on some rules. But the difference in business is that you are in more control than you think.

The rules of the game can always be changed. You do not have to approach the market the same way as everyone else. Can you find a way to build a product in a cheaper, faster way? Are there better ways to reach the customers that allows you to deliver to more people? You can even change the entire game. In business you can decide that if your approach is not working, you can re-orient the business to go after something completely different. There is no one there to stop you.

If you are losing in the game of business, then you simply change the rules of the game. If you still cannot win, then change the game. Those are the skills I didn't learn in business school.

TAKEAWAYS:

1. Three traits for a highly successful individual include perseverance, loyalty, and the courage to have a big idea.

2. Failure is not only an option—it is sometimes an inevitable outcome of decisions that you make.

3. The biggest regret you will ever have is not trying.

4. When you feel you are losing the game, change the rules. If that does not work, change the game. Remember you are in charge of your own decisions.

TWO

IT'S ALL ABOUT YOU

(SO YOU BETTER KNOW YOURSELF)

Only you can define your success. It can't be defined by an external group of people determining whether or not you are a success. It has to be defined by you. But the only way you can do that is to come to the understanding and appreciation that success has to be *all about you*. It has to be about your *self*. It's the only way you're going to be able to deliver the passion, the motivation, the energy, and the excitement to push through some of the enormous obstacles you're inevitably going to experience in your business and your professional career.

DO YOU KNOW YOU?

If you want to achieve a goal in your career or in your life, you have to become aware of why you're pursuing it. Success *has* to be all about you. While this may come across as egotistical or selfish, it is actually the most humbling way to be self-reflective or introspective. Only then can you recognize what you really want and what you're trying to achieve. The more you accept who you are and what you're trying to accomplish as part of your own vision and your goals, the better. It will allow you to be able to drive toward that outcome.

At the end of the day, when you go home utterly exhausted, you want to be able to look in the mirror and say, "I made the right decision." There are many distractions on any given day that can steer you away from your goals. If you can clearly identify for yourself what you want out of life, where your priorities are, and where your professional world interfaces with your personal life, only then can you create a framework to make decisions about what's key to your goals and when you should be willing to make a sacrifice to strive for those goals.

In his book *Idealized Design*, Russ Ackoff talks about framing the perfect state of a product or a concept. It's intended to be a product-oriented development book. But if you apply his treatise to the concept of an ideal state of being, it will help you focus on removing yourself from all the "noise" going on in your life and creating an ideal state of "you" in as much detail as possible. Once you do that, you can step back and look at how to steer yourself to achieve that ideal state.

Where a lot of people get jammed up is when they start with where they are today instead of with the ideal state. That creates obstacles that seem impossible to overcome to get to their own ideal state. For example, when many people struggle with climbing the corporate ladder, they find ways to convince themselves that they cannot get there. Whether it's their perceived lack of education, their inability to access the right network of people, or simply that life gets in the way, people create obstacles, perceived or real, to accomplishing their goals. When I talk to students and mentees I tell them to try and create the ideal state in their own minds, to think about what they want to be and the perfect place for them to be in the world. Once they are firm in their vision, then they can start making the decisions needed to achieve their goals.

One thing I try to impress on these students and mentees is that regardless of what your career path is, you have to come to the fundamental understanding that it absolutely has to be all about you. That's the hardest thing for them to grasp. It's not easy to understand what you are all about. Too often people go out and chase dreams for reasons not related to their goals. They chase the dreams they've been told to chase, or they get caught up in the career they're in right now and lose sight of what they were trying to accomplish.

If you want to be a CEO, then act like a CEO. If you want to be an entrepreneur, then you need to act like an entrepreneur. It's an issue of being tuned in to what it means to be you. Do you want to work in a large company? Or do you prefer to work in a small boutique? Are you motivated by achieving financial status? Do you want to be constantly innovating? Do you need security? Do you like a routine every day or do you want to reinvent yourself every five minutes? Do you want to be on the brink of the greatest innovation in the world? Or would you rather be incrementally changing things day by day?

ENVISION YOUR IDEAL STATE

Some people like risks, some people don't. Some people enjoy the excitement and adrenaline rush of starting a business, and some people don't. It doesn't mean that one is right and the other is wrong. It just means that you need to understand yourself.

In order to do so, you need to consider questions as specific as:

- What kind of work environment are you surrounded by?
- What kinds of people do you like to work with? How many hours do you want to work?
- What do you like to do once you leave work?

- Do you see yourself driving out to the countryside to go home to a little cottage when you get off from work, or would your perfect place be in a penthouse in a skyscraper?

Don't worry—there are no wrong answers. They are only the right answers for you.

Once you start identifying the answers to those questions, you might start realizing that perhaps material things aren't that important to you. Maybe you prefer to focus on social responsibilities. By going through exercises like this, you can start framing the basics of your decisions around what you really want out of life.

You can take it a step further by laying out the ideal state of what your family life would be:

- What is your work-life balance tolerance?

- Do you have children?

- Are you motivated by material wealth?

Those answers can help you frame a decision in your own mind that if you're going to attain a "house on the hill with a white picket fence," you will need to make X amount of money, which means you will have to make certain business or career decisions and sometimes make sacrifices to that end as well.

Let's take it even further.

Do you want to go to work in a pair of jeans, baggy sweatshirt, and flip-flops?

Do you want to build mobile apps and hang around with people who are working in an innovative, Google-type environment?

If that's the case, then you probably don't want to become a corporate executive in the defense industry, because that's not what they do. If you work in the defense industry, you'll be wearing dark blue power suits and sitting in conference rooms at meetings all day.

The more you can clearly identify what it is about yourself that you consider an ideal state, and the more you are truly confident and comfortable with that, the more honest you can be with yourself and understand what it going to take in hard work and sacrifice to reach your ambitions. It's wonderful when you can make those trade-offs and realize that's how you're going to frame your business. In this way, you make your business about *you*, and you don't allow the external environment and outside factors to manipulate your business into becoming something you don't want it to be. The more you're aware of yourself and what you want to achieve, the more likely it is that you will ultimately achieve your goals.

There are preconceived notions that people create in their minds about work, like the idea that showing up and doing the job well will automatically get you promoted. Unfortunately for many people, life gets in the way, and they wind up in the monotony of working every day while the clock ticks and the weeks and years go by, and then they look around and wonder why they are not in charge or why they are not achieving their goals.

What they fail to understand is that the only way to change their destiny is to have a solid vision of where they want to head. They need to start believing in who they want to become and start acting like that person. If they can create this ideal state where they think they should be, then they can start making decisions about how they're actually going to get there. Too many of us just wind up on the treadmill of life and don't sit down and look at what we *want* to do.

Often when I talk to students about the ideal state in detail, they get caught up in the next flavor of what they could be doing. They simply state that they want to move from being a member of a team to being the team leader or manager. They're not truly creating a specific environment of an ideal state for themselves. For instance, they're just deciding to change to a new job because they don't like what they're doing now. Well, that's not going to fix the problem. If you want a new job, you can get one, but unless you understand at your core what you want to be, you're still going to be unsatisfied in that new job. Are you a big risk taker? Do you love really fast-paced environments, or do you prefer a quiet and sedated workplace? Again, there isn't any right answer. It's only the answer *you* have that matters. Don't worry that it will never be perfect. As life evolves, your ideal state will mature along with your needs and views on life, and that is okay. Remember it is the journey, not the destination, that gets you to success as you define it.

So how do you know when you've achieved success? It's humbling to sit back and look at yourself and identify who you are, what you can achieve, where you want to go, and how you want to get there and to incrementally make those changes every day. In the process, you may realize that for you to do the things you want, you will have to sacrifice other things. At that point, you may also realize the sacrifice isn't worth it to you.

For example, you love to watch your kids play soccer and you want to be involved in their school. That's all well and good, but you can't work eighteen hours a day, six days a week and still do that. Thus you need to come up with a trade-off, and that's the step most individuals don't take. They don't consider the trade-off. They just keep climbing the career ladder without thinking. Then one day they realize they're trapped in a certain job or lifestyle because of their career progression. Financially, they have a mortgage to pay and car payments to make, and in order to make those nuts they end up *not* living the life they set out for themselves. They become hijacked by a culture that pushes them to achieve but doesn't give them the opportunity to express what they want to do. And if you don't have that ability to identify what you want to do, you're going to blink and life will have passed you by. The more you can try to achieve that perfect, ideal state you define for yourself, the better you'll be able to come to grips with who you are and where you're going to go and develop as a person.

Take another example: let's say you want to network and be heavily involved with your peers at the office. Then you have to get yourself out there. Don't be upset about the fact that nobody knows you if you don't actually participate in any social events. To be part of the office network, you have to go to the birthdays, the happy hours, and the office parties. Once you understand that, it will help propel you toward your goals.

Conversely, maybe you just want to work forty hours a week and be heavily involved in your family or church or community. If you have the self-confidence to say, "My work is a means to an end because life is more than just work to me," then you can do that. And this is often the point where people misplace their vision and what they're trying to become. As a businessperson, once you create a business there's a point where the business becomes your identity and you have difficulty separating the business from yourself or the other way around. You run the risk of becoming too egotistical about the fact that you can't be replaced or that you're too important to the business, and that's a dangerous place to be.

REEVALUATE: ARE YOU REALLY WHERE YOU WANT TO BE?

As you go back and constantly do this self-evaluation of your ideal state, to look at where you are going or what you want to become, you can make the business decisions to achieve the next chapter in your life. This reevaluation is vital because your ideal state always changes. It always evolves.

On a personal level, I learned this the hard way. As a student, I had a vision about what I was going to become, but I didn't appreciate the sacrifice it would take to get there. I wasn't the greatest student in the world, and I had competing priorities. For me it was a choice between studying and being in a very social party atmosphere, working in the bar business. Since the bar was more fun to me than studying, I would choose to work in the bar rather than stay home on a Friday night with a study group.

It wasn't until the tail end of my undergraduate years that I first started appreciating this. I realized that no one was going to hire me as a medical research assistant, because my grades simply weren't good enough. I started looking at the practical side of what I could do.

That's when I became a paramedic in the fire department. I also helped run a pediatric clinic and then an allergy practice. Through those experiences I recognized that I was not willing to sacrifice the rest of my twenties to achieve my goal of becoming a doctor.

At that point, my dad and I started STS, which was a great learning experience and a new environment for me. Every day I was learning something new and learning it on my own. It was eye opening, and I think the excitement for me came when we nailed down our first large program under my direction as program manager. I found that I liked what I was doing, *and* I was good at it.

That's where my skill was, taking something that was considered chaotic and creating a framework around it. I was then able to make it manageable and understandable and communicate that to the rest of the team. I had found my value and my niche.

You have to become very self-aware if you want to be an entrepreneur or enter any type of business leadership, because at the end of the day, even though you may be surrounded by teams, it can be very lonely. Those employees don't care how stressed you are in making a decision, they just want to know that you're going to make the decision in their best interest.

To be able to have that clarity in thought, to know why you're doing what you're doing and why you're making the sacrifices you're making for rewards you may or may not ever attain, you have to know who you are.

TAKEAWAYS:

1. Who are you? The more you can accept who you are and what you're trying to accomplish as part of your own vision and goals, the easier it will be to shape your future.

2. Clearly identify your idealized state—this will lead you to a better understanding of your sustainable business models.

3. Your reward may be the journey, so you have to want to be on this journey. If you're not able to get satisfaction out of the relentless pursuit of the ideal state, you're going to miss out. There's not always going to be a pot of gold at the end of the rainbow, so you have to enjoy the adventure all the way through.

THREE

BUSINESS PLANS ARE OVERRATED

(AND HERE'S WHY)

Business plans are a staple of business schools. They are promoted as inherently necessary for businesses. From the business owner's perspective, the creation of a business plan allows for the forming of a framework and a vision of how he or she sees the business operating. It also outlines the value add or product that is being offered to potential customers, and it can target and identify your customer segments. But the reality is that most business plans don't stand up to the realities of the market. They're created in a vacuum, constructed by staff or experts gathered in a room to provide input.

THE MARKET HAS SPOKEN

The truth is that the market, not your business plan, is going to define how your customers are going to accept your product. So while you can create the concept in a business plan, you still have to go out and test the waters and then go back and revisit your business plan to adapt it. I've yet to see any company over the last twenty years meet the goals of their business plan as it was originally laid out. It always takes a couple of years to experiment with business offerings and how they are going to provide the value add and discriminators to set themselves apart. My experience is that at least 50 percent of the companies I have worked with have shifted their model dramatically from their original business plan after five years.

In that light, I can't help but feel that business schools, and businesses themselves, place too much emphasis on having a business plan and a business model. To rely on a document to define a dynamic organization that will evolve based on market conditions, the economy, and customers' needs is like trying to force something to occur that is just not going to be effective for a growing business. So while having a business plan on paper may help you understand what you are trying to accomplish, it is possible to spend too much time on the analytics and details of that plan, missing the entire dynamic of what you're aspiring for, which is a customer to buy your product.

UNDERSTANDING THE INTENDED PURPOSE OF CREATING YOUR BUSINESS PLAN

Over the course of your career, you will eventually have to create a business plan for someone. You will need one to get a loan from a bank or to explain to investors what you need their money for. Or maybe you will need to develop one for your boss at work in order to get the next project started. Regardless, the focus in a business needs to be on managing risks and driving outcomes.

When you're creating a business plan, you first need to understand your audience. Too often, business owners use their business plans to reach the wrong audience. They're either trying to convince themselves or others why they're good or trying to argue their position of why their service or product is best—instead of creating a document that defines a model and strategy that is executable.

For example, if you're a business owner looking for partners or investors, you will need a business plan with analytics to show how your business will actually be profitable. So that is one audience. But that plan may not necessarily translate into a model that will lend itself to actual execution. So while the business plan as taught in business school will talk about return on investment and net present value, the truth is that no one ever makes the race to revenue as soon or as profitably as they predict.

In a real-life example, a former associate and business owner purchased an existing business and rebranded it and expanded it to a life long dream of the perfect business. Unfortunately the deal was created without a full understanding of the original business concept and what all the other stakeholders wanted out of the business. Their business plan explained that the existing business would be used as a platform to expand from its current offerings to new lines of business. Unfortunately, the plan for the business expansion was created in a vacuum and was not based in the reality of what it was going to take to evolve and expand. This resulted in overpromising in an effort to respond to too many customers and underachieving as a business and ultimately failing financially. The business owner took money from personal investors using the 3F model: friends, family, and fools. In the end, she simply did not spend sufficient time figuring out what was executable under the original business model. The whole adventure was lose:lose all the way around. The new business never made it and all the investors lost.

If you're measuring yourself against the plan rather than against the execution, you're not going to be able to define whether you are truly advancing to where you need to get or whether you've achieved your milestones. You have to be able to ask yourself: "Have I reached a point where the business plan is executing in accordance with the way I want it to execute?" If it is not, are you able to allow the market to influence you to redirect that business?

There's a tremendous discrepancy between what managers think of as a business plan, which is a large document with all this information on target markets and segments and revenues, and what their company's strengths, weaknesses, opportunities, and threats (SWOT) analysis may be. They simply don't spend enough time on the execution plan. And in today's market, that's going to be an enormous challenge because the majority of new higher-paying jobs currently are coming out of large businesses, not small businesses. At most small businesses, total employment falls off after the first five years, assuming they are still in business.

BUSINESS PLAN VS. EXECUTABLE PLAN

It's important to understand the difference between a business plan and an executable plan because the current market environment is not going to stand forever. Eventually, the availability of capital is going to shrink. It's going to be harder and harder to get $10 million for an app you created over the weekend. It's going to be even more difficult to jump-start a business around a potential product that has not even started to monetize itself yet. The fact that *you* think your product is going to be the next Facebook or Instagram will not be enough. All of a sudden it's going to be about the execution. And the reality is business schools are not spending any significant time teaching their students how to execute in a business. Why the discrepancy? Quite frankly, it's not sexy. It's far more exciting to talk about products and their applications. The companies that created them have received huge valuations. The fact that many of these companies are not making any money years down the road gets brushed aside.

Then the questions are going to be, is your business a sound business that's able to execute when times get tough? Do you have strong management skills? Have you found the right people who will make up your core team?

You can have brilliant technology, a creative concept, a generous offering, or a fabulous service, but at the end of the day you have to have the right people in place to be able to execute your business at the right price. Because if the idea is executable but you have a dysfunctional management team, you're never going to be able to execute the idea to its fullest potential.

So having an emphasis on the team, the engine that's going to run the business, is as important, if not more important, than the actual idea or the technology being offered. There are thousands of businesses that start up every day that have great ideas and concepts with dynamic plans and vision for the future. Some of them may even be very well funded. But they lack an adequate understanding of how to manage the program or how to execute a business plan. There's a tendency to run back and look at the plan and just continue to update it. The definition of insanity is doing the same thing over and over again and expecting a different result. There's a lot of that kind of modeling, where managers go back to a business plan as opposed to comprehending that sometimes it's just about sheer hard work and perseverance and not about your plan telling you that you are wrong. It's that you're not executing the plan in the right manner. You have to go back and readdress, realign, and sometimes completely pivot the business and realize that the sweeter part of the market for you is at the higher end or the lower end. It may be that you need to reduce the quantity of what you're trying to push out because that's what will drive new interest as customers look at your product differently. Those are the kinds of things that most business plans miss.

In our case, STS never had a formalized, detailed business plan. The reality of the situation was—and this is typical of how a lot of companies start out—we came up with a concept of what we were going to offer, we did an initial budget, we targeted customers that potentially would buy our product, and then we just jumped in. All of a sudden, we had to create documents, cash flow and income statements, to provide information to the banks and investors in order to get loans and lines of credit.

Granted, in today's economy, there is a push for the dream of creating another "unicorn": another mythical company with an astronomical valuation in comparison to both the initial investment and annual revenues. These unicorn companies are quite common these days: Uber, Airbnb, and Snapchat are some examples.

In most of our pursuits at STS, we had a concept, but it was more of a program that we were managing. We started a company with a product idea that we were managing against that budget. We were simultaneously in pursuit of development of that product and constrained by our budget, which taught us how to execute. Then, as that product came to the end of its life cycle (or sometimes it was a product that we couldn't get traction on in the market), we would pivot. I think one of the other things that is often missed is that there is a typical bell curve in which a product life cycle occurs. If you wait too long, when a product starts to go through its life cycle and begins the downward or the backward side of the curve, it's very hard to jump to the next product because you lose momentum, resources, funding, and customer attention. It becomes very hard to then sell this next product.

Remember the example of the biometrics program in chapter 1. STS had a great new opportunity to develop and mature an entire business line that had been untapped. Based on market circumstances and US national interests, a huge amount of funding was coming out of the federal government for this business. We thought we had made it. We had a tremendous program with great opportunity. What we did not appreciate were the market forces at work. We spent too much time looking inward at growth rather than in pursuit of new opportunities and new customers. As we reached the highest point of our growth, we did not even realize that we were starting to slide down that curve. We had no significant new customers and contracts coming in, but we thought we were okay because we were infatuated with our current success. Soon the curve became steeper and steeper, and our revenue fell off almost overnight. Going uphill is a lot harder than going down. But if you start going down too fast, inevitably you will fall to the bottom. And I can tell you it hurts . . . a lot . . . as I have fallen more than once.

Having the timing to know when your next product or next offering needs to be implemented in the midst of getting traction on your existing product is a hard lesson to learn. You cannot simply teach it. It is a skill like understanding the big picture—it takes time and experience, and you may learn some very hard lessons along the way.

It's not necessarily just about expanding; it's also about opening up the opportunities to create revenue. And when you get an uptick of revenue, there's typically a growth in infrastructure or personnel or facilities or other resources required to run your business as well. But when that revenue goes away, you've already purchased that infrastructure, so you either have to scale back, which is painful, or you have to sit and wait and hope you're able to gain new revenue.

Again, what I am saying is that you need to shift away from a business plan that says, *I'm going to offer X, Y, and Z to this customer,* to a model that asks, *How am I going to be able to execute my business?*

If you need ten new customers, then you need to be able to bid X number of contracts. It has to be measurable against an execution strategy, so that you know you are hitting these milestones. It all goes back to the execution and not back to a plan to create the product and convince people that it is right. You want to be able to achieve a milestone that you can actually manage against.

The key is to bring it down to something that is relevant to the audience. You have to assume that the audience is not as technically competent or aware of your industry and your offering as you are, so you need to be able to distill that information down and explain it to them. That's a difficult thing to do.

Focus on the strategies you will put in place to ensure that this business you are going to invest your own money in or ask others to invest in will actually make revenue and be profitable. Defend why that's going to happen. Do not say that it's going to be the next iPhone. No one really cares about that. Outline how you will do it, how you will make the distribution, how you will displace your competitors. Identify why your concept will actually work.

The main thing for you to understand is exactly what are you in business for, because once you fully understand that, you have a better chance of executing your plan successfully. As a business owner, you have to understand what you are truly selling and what makes you different from everyone else out there. There are very few places where a new company is able to enter the market today and be completely different and unique. Those kinds of products come by once in a generation. As a start-up it's next to impossible to generate them, because it takes a tremendous amount of funding. It also takes an entire marketing machine and a whole supply chain infrastructure to roll that kind of new product out globally. Can it be done? Sure. It's just more challenging to do in today's environment because if the big guys see you as a competitor, they will find ways to buy you, block you, outpace you, outmarket you, or outsell you.

Even at the small local level or the regional level where you're trying to sell your product, you're still going to have competition from all sides that will try to dilute your ability to enter the market. The opposition is worried that your place in the mix will compromise their positions and their revenues. You need to be cognizant of why you are different from the person next to you, your competitors. And you have to be able to distinguish yourself through your relationship with the customer by clearly delineating what your value proposition is so that they really understand and feel that you are servicing their needs. Again, business plans do not intrinsically focus on the other end of the transaction—the customer.

Business plans are typically oriented to what you are offering and how that will generate revenue, what your growth trajectories are, and what your return on revenues will be. But the reality is, the customer is the one who pays the bills for you when you're selling your product. When you are able to incorporate the customer's feedback and address it and subsequently realign your business priorities internally so that you can service that client, that's when you will start making traction and making yourself sustainable to enterprise. If you don't have customers yet, take every opportunity to observe and ask questions of everyone who might be able to give you an opinion. Some of the greatest insight can come from someone who has no technical understanding of your business.

If you do not understand where your position is in the market space, you will lose the opportunity to have a clear framework. If you do not understand your own internal framework as to how you want your business to be operating and what you want out of your business, you will become paralyzed when a decision is presented to you. With a framework, you have the ability to make decisions based on what you are offering today and how that will impact your business tomorrow. You can't remain focused on what you are doing today and the fact that you are doing it well without considering the implications of that product or that customer going away in the next few years. You must consider how you are going to reinvent your business and expand into other areas.

This applies across the full line of businesses, not just technology-based enterprises. Look at owners of plumbing businesses, or an HVAC enterprise, or small construction companies. Plumbing is still plumbing, an electrician is still an electrician. But the market constantly gets disrupted by someone who comes in and finds a more innovative way to do it cheaper, who finds a new way to reach more clients than you can, who figures out how to make their delivery that much more effective to potential customers. Although the core skill trade of being an electrician or a plumber hasn't changed, how that service is delivered to a customer can change. If you're not paying attention, and you're not looking at continuous ways to innovate your service offering, you're going to be constrained by what the market will allow you to have, and other companies will compete to take your share.

Now you understand the workings of an open market. Others are going to continuously compete, and you don't have any right to think that you deserve a piece that should be yours. There will always be somebody else out there looking to start his or her own business. In that context, you have to look at what the market will offer you and have the confidence to absorb the risk to adjust your business model. You need to be able to look at the new offering, to make a change, to take opportunities when they come to you—and be willing to embrace that change and jump into the next opportunity as it's presented. That's the only way you're going to continuously grow.

But again, in order to see what the market is presenting to you, you can't be caught up in the day to day of looking at your business plan or the balance sheet or the profit and loss statement and trying to manage through that plan. You can't get stuck looking at your business plan and believing you will be profitable at the end of the year when everything else is telling you that you are losing money. You need to have something you can *execute* against, not *manage* against, and often you don't learn that in business school.

TAKEAWAYS:

1. The market, not your business plan, is going to define how your customers are going to accept your product.

2. It's important to understand the difference between a business plan and an executable plan. You need to shift away from a business plan that merely offers the customer a product to a plan that asks and clearly answers how you are going to be able to execute your business.

3. You must understand your own internal framework and how you want your business to operate.

4. At the end of the day you will be measured by how well you deliver. Focus your effort on a plan of action on how you will execute rather than evaluating progress against a notional business plan that does not take into account the flexibility and responsiveness needed to be sucessful.

FOUR

IT'S BETTER TO BE KNOWN THAN GOOD

(BUT GOOD HELPS TOO)

There's an old saying that it's better to be lucky than good. Well, I have a different take on that. I say it's better to be known than good. An interesting thing about STS and the growth we've experienced and the opportunities we've successfully been able to capture and develop into long-term, sustainable business models and opportunities is that it wasn't necessarily the product or the idea that made STS successful.

NETWORK, NETWORK, NETWORK

Rather, it was an understanding of our place in the business environment, the marketplace, and our ability to generate connections with customers who felt we were a value add based on the fact that they knew us and respected us. Those relationships allowed us to open up new business lines, whether it was the medical simulation side, the work we were developing with body armor systems, or our secure communications business.

We always had a known group of people and companies that we'd worked with successfully in the past, and we reached out to them again and again as we developed new opportunities for a new market. Some were merely contacts. Others were what the market presented to us with regard to opportunity concepts and products. Regardless of which avenue they came to us, the fact that we were able to move quickly and effectively in business wasn't always linked to having an innovative product or a fantastic concept that we then had to go out and market and sell. When you have to venture out and market or sell those new products, you need an avenue or an opportunity to present those goods to market, whether it's to the individual customer or into some large distribution via media or the Internet.

One factor people fail to learn in business school is the staggering importance of understanding the power of networking. Every person and every business has a network where there's commerce going on among all the little points in that network. It extends beyond just a business and your personal life. It grows to the greater network of people that you deal with. Then it fans out to the businesses you intersect with and then to an enterprise. From there the connections should continue to grow and grow.

When you look at most business schools, they do a good job of teaching you about social networking, public speaking, and other components of what it takes to be a successful businessperson, but they don't talk a lot about selling. To be established and relevant in a network, you have to sell yourself. Sure, just showing up is half the battle, but the other half is to be relevant and respected in that network. To do that, you have to offer yourself up as a branded product that people trust and want to be associated with.

As I mentioned, for some reason the four-letter word "sell" doesn't echo in the halls of most business schools. But as an entrepreneur you are *always* selling, and you need to recognize that your next customer or your next opportunity could be a random event. It could be the person you meet at a restaurant and start a conversation with or the guy you greet at a random happy hour. It could even be someone you run into at the neighborhood grocery store. Any one of them might be your next customer. Or it could be someone in the network you've cultivated.

I have to admit networking has always been a hard task for me. I can hold a great one-on-one conversation about an important topic, or I can hold a room of hundreds of people captive on a topic I know very little about. But ask me to work a networking event to meet new people and you might as well ask me to pull out my own teeth. So I found it easier to make direct, intimate contacts, one person at a time. It was a lot harder and obviously took a longer time, but it worked for me. If I can do it, then you can do it, too.

LISTEN, LEARN, CONNECT

So how do you become known? I encourage everyone, students or employees, to take every meeting at every opportunity. If you have an opportunity for a professional and/or social meeting with a potential client, a peer, a potential vendor, or even a competitor in a respectful, transparent, open environment, start mapping that out. Don't miss the chance, because even if that person is not your customer or your resource, he or she might be able to connect you to someone who is. If you sit down and start engaging with people in your network and asking questions, not in an annoying manner and not asking for favors, but engaging to learn, you'll find out very quickly that you're not that far away from those customers or resources that you may need.

And it's not necessarily always about finding a customer. You don't want to be running around asking friends of friends to come buy your product or use your service. If you do that, you will very quickly find yourself being minimized or excluded. If you present yourself as a person who is always trying to sell, people will see you as lowering the value of your brand, and you will become a commodity. That is a very big danger.

I emphasize to students, mentees, and my staff that in order to develop respect you have to be responsive. If somebody asks for a meeting or you ask for a meeting, unless there is some legitimate, significant reason that you cannot take the meeting, attend. Go.

When you meet with somebody, typically you are both figuratively sitting across the table looking at each other. Your goal is to eventually turn yourself around so that you are both on the same side of the table, allowing for a shared point of view of the same problem or opportunity. It's no longer you looking at opposite ends of an elephant and trying to describe it. You're now both looking at the same problem on the same piece of paper, from the same orientation, and trying to address it. The faster you can get to that side of the table, the better off you're going to be and the more your client will trust you.

It sounds rogue because it's the antithesis to what everyone says you're supposed to do. You're supposed to target your client base. You're supposed to have a discriminator against your competition. You're supposed to have detailed intimacy about what your customer wants so that you can use that information.

I don't necessarily disagree with any of that; I just have an issue with the execution principles. People spend far too much time delving into the detail of customers and segments and how they're going to integrate that into marketing campaigns. But when you're a small business and what you're selling is your reputation, you have to actually produce on that reputation. You have to give people evidence on that reputation. The reality is that you are not in a position to make your market. You're a market taker, not a market maker. You have to respond to what signals the market is giving you based on demand. If a demand signal is that you have to be cheaper and faster than your competitors, then that's what you need to be. If a demand signal is that you need to be more flexible with what you are offering as a small business, that's what you need to be.

That's the way we have constructed STS. It has been a challenge over time to keep a lower overhead and remain agile and flexible in our responses. As the company scales, those are wonderful words to say but very hard to keep in play. Again, our benefit is that STS has a deliberately small network of trusted peer companies that we work with intimately. With a small, tight group we can leverage each other to move forward in our best interests.

In addition to the peer companies, my network includes a large group of people with a variety of expertise. Within this group of people I know I can reach out to somebody and say, "Hey, I need a favor. Do you know such and such? This person? Do you have a referral inside this organization?" With the diversity of backgrounds you can get some unique insight from someone who may be an "outsider" and provide a unique perspective.

Within one or two touch points, I'll get the referral that I need in order to at least advocate for my position. I will get the name of someone to whom I could be a qualified supplier, or I can get a contact to present my case to be a subcontractor to someone on another opportunity. It's that reaching out to our network to get *beyond* our network that has led STS to continue to develop our success.

Today there is an entire generation growing up who never had to find a way to vocalize in order to be heard. They can simply post on Facebook and immediately hit a thousand of their friends and tell them what they need. As this generation is fast becoming our next group of business leaders, there will be a very interesting dynamic whereby people who grew up in that model will generate social media followings and have an audience pay attention to them. The challenge in this model, though, is that they will only be able to hold the audience's attention for a very short period of time.

In either model, the only way you can consistently get repeat business is to deliver on what you say you're going to deliver. At the end of the day, you still have to make a sale to an individual. There's still another person on the other end buying your product. You still have to be able to convince that person to separate with their money to pick up your service or product. The only way you're going to be able to do repeat business is if you do what you say you're going to do and deliver on time—and do it every single time. Be there on time with exactly what you promised to deliver. Only then will people start paying more attention to you. Only then will they truly know you are trustworthy and respectable. Only then will they know they are going to receive continued high-quality service from you. Only then will they continue to come back to you. At that point, they will know they don't have to go out and find that service or product again. They will know when they need something to call *you*.

YOUR PERSONAL BRAND SHOULD BE LIKE WATER—CLEAR AND TRANSPARENT

Your brand must be transparent to you, to your staff and your customers. It has to be part of the culture that you bring into the company. If you're going to have the forward-facing people inside your organization deliver the message to the customers, they all have to believe it and they all have to be transparent about the brand. You can't have a perceived brand that you are trying to represent to the customer and not have the individuals who are selling or presenting that image to the customers believe in the brand. That becomes artificial, and people will see right through it. If you think of your company as a company of one, your brand, or what you're representing, has to be truly you, and it has to be transparent so that it is obvious to everyone that this is what you represent. You need to clearly identify the brand not only to yourself but also to the internal part of your organization. What is the brand that you are representing? How are you going to carry that brand forward? What do you need to be doing on a daily basis to accomplish that? For example, if a characteristic of your brand is responsiveness, then if somebody sends an email, you need to be sure that standards are set to define what is considered responsive and that everyone is trained to meet or exceed those standards. They need to be able to get the customer their answer as fast as they possibly can. Why? Because this is your brand. These are your values. This is what you represent every single day, all day.

This concept is crucial to being able to have a long-term sustainable model. It doesn't mean that over time your brand doesn't develop, mature, or even become completely reinvented, but that has to be a conscious choice. You can't present yourself as agile and responsive today and mature and robust tomorrow. You have to decide who you are and what you're doing. If you're a new company, perhaps your brand is, "I'm a start-up. I move fast. I create great product and do value add."

Identification of a brand goes back to what we talked about before, which is the ideal state. You can achieve your ideal state only after you have a framework for it in your own mind. Then you can represent that this is the ideal company, and this is the ideal state where you want your company to be in five years, ten years, or fifteen years. That will help you identify what your brand needs to be.

As an example, you can say, "I want to be the universal supplier of X, Y, and Z." Maybe that means you have to be a low-cost model. If you need to be a low-cost model, then you know that in your ideal state this is what your organization needs to look like. It has to be very flat. It has to be very transparent. It has to be very agile. It can't have a lot of overhead. You can set all that up once you know what you want your vision of your company to be.

Most successful companies that I've seen end up, after about five years or so, establishing a nice rhythm of what their business is. When you ask a business owner what she *thought* she would be doing at the five-year mark versus what she is *actually* doing, there's likely going to be a pretty big discrepancy between the two. No doubt she tried a bunch of ideas that didn't work. As a result, her company pivoted based on what was being presented by the market. They probably were presented new opportunities and jumped in, resulting in an evolution of their current business offerings. Businesses will continue to evolve because there are very few models and products that stand the test of time. Even large industries, like the automotive industry, continue to have to reinvent every several years with new products and new offerings.

Bottom line, the customer has to know you and like you. Just because your brand is known doesn't necessarily translate to sales, specifically for start-ups. Just because you see people spending millions of dollars on ads doesn't necessarily mean those ads are translating into real-time revenue.

What does translate into sales is when people know you are a reputable person to work with—when you actually do what you say you are going to do. That carries throughout any industry. You would think this notion is nothing new. People have known this for years. You would think that entrepreneurs would automatically focus on being disciplined and staying engaged. But too often they do not. Too often they make a random phone call and think that they've tried and nobody is interested. You have to *stay* engaged. You have to try repeatedly. You have to stay positive, and you have to stay motivated. Your brand and your identity can't change between your first interaction and your seventh.

Go back and apply this to being the new kid on the block. Remember the very first day you showed up in school? In my case, I was a military brat. Every two to three years, I was in a new school. Being the new kid, it takes a while to make friends. It takes a while to understand the dynamics, to identify who the troublemakers are and who the fun kids are. It takes a few weeks to weed out who you're going to align yourself with.

The same thing applies in business. When you show up with a new product you've created, you're the new kid on the block. You're a new entrant. You're going to have to put yourself out there. The more you place yourself in the group of people that you want to engage with, the more accepting and more welcoming they are going to be.

In order to be successful, you need to be very clear on what you're trying to provide and then associate yourself with other people who are contributory to what you're trying to accomplish. Align them as part of your portfolio of business partners. Not only will they help you propel your business forward, they will also send business your way when you help them.

Eventually what you'll find is that your collaborators will not only trust and respect you but will also defend you when you're not even there. It's very important for you to engage everyone as your peers so that you can rely on them as another asset, another resource that you have at your disposal.

A discrepancy that I see between what you learn in business school and real business practice is that business schools tend to present the market and the consumer as data points. The market is discussed as industry segments, trends, and analyses. Consumers are examined as inputs and statistics. What you don't often learn is that "the market" and "the consumer" require daily human interaction, fostering relationships with real people.

It's at that point that it's more important to be trusted and respected in a network than it is to have a brand that is just window dressing. If you don't have the reputation and relationship to be able to pick up the phone and call somebody—not send them an email, not run another radio spot, not put a Super Bowl ad out there—then it will be very hard to develop that lead into a real opportunity that you can actually gain revenue from.

TAKEAWAYS:

———————

1. You must sell yourself. Networking is critical and powerful. Listen to your customers. Learn from your experiences. Connect with peers and potential customers.

2. Your brand must be transparent, and—just as important— it must be embedded within your organization's culture.

3. The market and the consumer are not merely data points. They are real people, real decision makers that require a certain level of human cultivation.

———————

FIVE

WHEN A WINDOW OPENS

(WALK THROUGH IT)

One important factor that I can attribute to my own success that I wasn't taught in business school is how to discern whether a particular event is actually an open window of opportunity. Over time, I learned to be in a constant state of preparedness to identify or discern events of opportunity, the associated risks, and the length of time that I had to seize the opportunity and deliver a solution.

DISCERN YOUR OPPORTUNITY

A constant state of preparedness is what the military calls "situational awareness." It's a heightened sense of understanding of what's going on around you, of what's going on in the economy, and looking at where the opportunities lie. It could be events happening in the news or in a company's business. It could be a new contract or the loss of an existing contract. It could be hiring a new employee. These are all events where you can say, "Does this give me an opportunity or an advantage to move quickly, to get there before somebody else and get to that customer to potentially consider a change?"

Situational awareness is especially crucial for small businesses because a small business always has to be dynamic and agile in its ability to move. A large business is a behemoth with levels of bureaucracy and a strong market presence. Moving quickly to seize an opportunity may be more difficult. Large companies tend to be strategic in their thinking rather than tactical. However, if a large business does decide to move in a given direction, they are more likely to have sufficient resources to move, and it's very hard for a small business to compete with that. Smaller companies have the ability to outplay larger competitors by being aware of what's going on and moving faster to assess a potential opportunity and the inherent risks and to make a decision.

The number-one concept about discernment that you need to understand is that there *is* going to be an event. There will always be an event. It will happen whether you like it or not. It will happen when you're not prepared for it. So the more you understand what you're trying to accomplish and what you're trying to achieve in your ideal state of the business, the more likely that you will be able to act when the window opens—or even better, that you will be able to foresee the window opening and be there at the very front.

Central to this is the core understanding about yourself. This applies across the spectrum of business or the spectrum of life. It doesn't matter whether it's a business decision or a personal life decision. You need to understand yourself and what you're trying to accomplish at the core. Everybody's different, and everybody has their own priorities, and that doesn't mean that your priorities are right or wrong. It just means that they are *your* priorities. You have to be 100 percent confident that, as of today, this is what you believe in, and this is what you're trying to achieve as an individual. Once you understand the core of it, you need to understand how you fit into the ecosystem. And the more you're aware of that ecosystem, the more you're going to be able to spot these windows when they open.

ASSESS THE RISKS

Continuously having this "situational awareness" of what's going on around you and how it ties back to the ecosystem can work to your advantage when an event window presents itself. You have to understand what you want out of the business, what the business wants out of you, and where you're positioning the business to go. With this understanding, when an opportunity presents itself, you can move without hesitation. Eventually, as you refine your approach, you're able to see opportunities more instinctively and move without having to analyze the alternatives.

Don't be fooled—an opportunity doesn't always present itself as a momentous change. It can be a smaller change that you can drive through and make an impact on the way you're conducting business. Any type of event can provide you with that opportunity for change. But only those who are prepared to see that opportunity will be able to take the greatest advantage of it.

What happens too often is that people get mired in the details. They're overcome by the crisis du jour and become temporarily blind to a potential opportunity. The truth is, there is always going to be some level of crisis. So the more you are able to identify and address crises, the quicker you will be to resolve them.

This also applies inside an organization. If you're trying to move through a company to achieve a goal, to push your agenda, or to sell a new idea, when these events happen you have to be prepared to jump out and make a quick action, a dart or sprint, to get your momentum started. This allows you to take the people who are impacted by the event and show them the benefit of your solution. That way, they can consider following your opportunity rather than following the status quo or what they've been doing in the past.

SEIZING THE MOMENT

Understanding when that window of opportunity is going to open, how long it is going to stay open, and how big the opening is going to be is vital to being able to outmaneuver the competition. Consider these three strategies for seizing opportunities: (1) the beginning of the wave (the Trailblazer); (2) the peak of the wave (the Fast Follower); or (3) the back end of the wave (the Reactor).

The Trailblazer

Being the Trailblazer, or the First Mover, is great because you get in on the groundswell of what's going on, and everyone's going to start making changes. But if you're too far out in front, you can get crushed by the wave when it rolls over, or you could be so far in front that you won't enjoy the benefits of riding the wave, and you won't get anywhere near the potential opportunity you could with regard to revenue or dramatic change. In essence, Trailblazers are also at highest risk of failing first, with some documented estimates showing that almost half of all Trailblazers fail with their original business model.

The Fast Follower

Fast Followers are those who enter the market early but not first. A Fast Follower example that is often touted is Google. Yahoo was already in the search engine domain by the time Google launched, yet Google has gone on to have tremendous success. Studies have indicated that Fast Followers tend to achieve much greater long-term success.

The Reactor

The other alternative is being on the back of the wave and getting nothing at all. In that scenario, you're paddling really hard to at least get to the peak of the wave, but you've wasted a lot of energy and you're not going anywhere. There's nothing that you can really offer to distinguish yourself from the Fast Followers or the Trailblazers.

TIMING IS EVERYTHING

If you don't understand (or don't have the stomach for) the inherent risks of being a Trailblazer, it may not be in your best interest to be out in front of the wave.

Maybe it *would* be in your best interest to purposefully lag behind in the Fast Follower position. If you only want to get so far ahead because you want to position yourself for the next wave, then you can use that wave to your benefit and ride it through so that you can catch the next one. But if you're not aware of what you're trying to accomplish and where you're trying to drive the business, you'll be chasing the wrong wave. You'll be going after the wrong event window, or you won't be prepared at all because your nose will be buried in the books trying to make sure you're balancing out the projects so that you can be profitable.

Missing out on catching the right wave at the right time can hurt your business in multiple ways. I have learned this the hard way more than once. Many years ago we were fortunate to get a contract to develop a new security and surveillance concept for use by US forces. We were way ahead of the wave—by almost five years, in fact. As we developed the technology, we became so focused on what we were doing that we lost sight of the environment and the competition. We so fiercely defended building on our concepts that we never saw the competition circling around us. We were not in touch with the other potential customers.

Then it happened. The gates broke open, and the wave came rolling in. The Defense Department approved a multimillion-dollar contract in one year to procure the types of products we were building. The wave came in along with all the other competitors. And the waves kept coming year after year for the next five years. We got overrun.

One company that was not even in our space came into the market and simply bought up most of the suppliers so that they could build their own product. Overnight, they went from a nonentity to a dominant player in the market. We were the leading developer of our product, and still the customer opted to use another suppler. Even ten years later, our product outperforms the systems used today. But that does not matter, because we lost that battle. You have to be constantly prepared to move and react to the market when the window opens. If you are too narrowly focused you will miss out on your opportunity, no matter how good your product is.

This is something that's hard to learn in business school. It's difficult for schools to instill in you the ability to create an instinctual framework that relies on your understanding of the business and whether or not you should be taking action on this opportunity. To be honest, that's the Holy Grail of decision making: How do you execute a risk-based decision-making framework that's applicable across the board to all sorts of entities?

It's also one of the questions I am most often asked. How do I make my business decisions, and more pointedly, how do I know I am making the right business decisions? I think the reason I've been successful in the decisions I've made is that most of the time I'm not just looking for the upside of the decision. I'm also looking at whether my choice will crash and burn or whether the company will unravel because I may make a bad decision.

There will always be external events that enter into the decision-making process that you can't control. You're in a position to react rather than act. At that point, you're looking at "If I don't make this right decision, not only is it going to impact the company financially, it's going to impact all of the employees. It's going to impact the brand of the business. The employees may not be able to cash their paychecks, because financially it was a bad decision. And if that unravels, I won't be able to produce revenue, because I rely on my employees to be able to produce quality products and services to the customer."

When you have that level of emotional intensity in making a decision, you invest more into the decision-making process than what you might if you were just one of many in a business meeting adding your two cents' worth.

A good friend of mine—who is also a small business owner—once commented that, "If you don't lose sleep over your business, your business has already failed." What he meant was that if you don't create a framework for your decision process, you can't put it in context of how it's going to impact your business. Then it becomes not just a decision but an execution. And that's something that can be difficult to learn: how important executing a decision really is. Sometimes a decision is just a decision, but more often than not it's all about the execution and follow-through.

Too often business owners rely on analytical models or consultants to help them frame a decision when what they really need is simply the confidence to take the next step. As a business owner, you may not know what the right decision is, but you have to be able to *take* that next step to move forward. If you don't, the entire business becomes paralyzed. If your employees don't feel you have confidence in where you're going and what you need to do, your leadership begins to erode. Again, this is something you won't necessarily learn in business school. The realization that if you hold yourself a certain way you'll exude confidence to your staff, to your customers, and to your peers is more a skill you learn by doing. Over time, you will develop the confidence to make decisions. This doesn't mean you might not obsess about the decision on the inside, but you'll have the momentum to go forward.

Does this involve risk taking? Absolutely it does. Owning a business is all about risk. It's all about the management of risk and stepping forward beyond the normal level of risk taking. There have been many times over the last twenty years when we have gambled everything on a single decision. It was through our perseverance that we just kept pushing and refused to take no for an answer. We kept the momentum up and made some great accomplishments based on that alone.

We weren't the smartest people in the world. We weren't the most well-funded or the most well-connected. If you looked around, our peers thought they were in a better position than we were, and yet over the last ten years, a lot of them have gone out of business despite appearing to be more capable. What we did understand was how to discern an opportunity, how to assess the risks, and how to move quickly (or not move) in a very intense, risky environment.

Through these experiences, I learned several key lessons. Number one would be to build confidence in your decision-making ability. You have to realize you may not be the smartest person in the room, you may not be the most educated or the most experienced person in the room, but you have to have the confidence to know that you can still run with the crowd. If you work harder and better than anyone else, if you commit 120 percent without hesitation, you will deliver the right decision.

The second lesson goes hand in hand with confidence, and that is that you have to be able not only to manage risk but to be confident in managing the risk. You need to be able to look at a challenging situation, like an event window, and understand how to mitigate the risk. A lot of times, businesses lose sight of what they're trying to accomplish, and when you lose sight of what you're trying to accomplish, you start inserting other things into the risk. Being able to peel it all back and identify that objective, and then being able to mitigate the potential ramifications of making that decision, takes practice and confidence.

The third lesson is that you have to understand what the purpose of your business is. It's easy to spend too much time on mission and vision and values statements at the business-ownership level or at the executive-management level. While there's definitely a purpose and a reason to have a mission and vision statement, there's much more to explain to the team about what you're trying to accomplish.

What an executive leader and what a business owner are trying to accomplish are very different things. As I describe in my first book, *Chasing the White Rabbit: A Discovery of Leadership in the 21st Century*, executive leaders can become overly focused on esoteric statements that are really meaningless to the operation of a business. As a business owner, you have to be able to look in the mirror and have a true understanding of what you're trying to accomplish. Once you understand that, then all the other decisions about risk become so much more straightforward, because now you know why you're doing it and what the end state is going to be. You know what you're trying to gain out of the business, and that helps frame every decision you make in the future.

STS does a lot of international work. A majority of our work right now is defense related, so it's important for me to be very attuned to events going on around the world. Listening to what Congress has to say, or listening to what military leaders are talking about, sets us up not just for tomorrow but possibly for the next five years. We know that every couple of years Congress is going to turn over, and the White House is going to turn over every four to eight years. There are always going to be new things that we need to be aware of so that we can identify those opportunities.

There are always demand signals that come out from the marketplace or from your industry that allow you to reasonably predict what's going to happen next. This is especially true on the large business side, where they are required to have so much exposure based on their stock. If it's a publicly traded company, you can access all of this information. There's a tremendous amount of data that you can glean from quarterly reviews. When you examine all that data, you can see the bigger picture of where the business or company is going.

From our standpoint, we have a pretty different business model than most in that the closer somebody is aligned to us as a valued partner, the more transparent we are to them. Probably more so than any of our competitor companies or peer companies would be in the same situation. We're very transparent about the opportunities of revenue that we are pursuing. And we do that simply because if they are a valued partner, what are we trying to hide from them? If they are a partner with STS, then our success is going to be their success, and they're going to want to work with us because we're going to continue to include them in our success.

If you're insular and closed, and you're not willing to communicate and cooperate and collaborate with other partners, then when you need the help, when you need the intel of what's going on around you that you do not have, your peers may not be willing to share. And that information might be crucial to you when an event window opens.

The most difficult part of seizing windows of opportunity is being honest with yourself about the amount of risk that you're willing to tolerate to try to effect change. Are you willing to be the Trailblazer? Are you willing to be the Fast Follower? Or are you willing to pass up the opportunity because it may be wasting money, time, or energy? If you don't know what you're trying to achieve, you're going to make the decision to go after every opportunity that opens, and then you run the risk of failing at first or just failing.

You need to be selective. The only way you can do that is to have a firm footing of where you'll be able to push forward through obstacles because pushing through these windows of opportunity isn't necessarily a pain-free or no-cost option. You may have to make additional investments or sacrifices in some other area because you've pursued this challenge. Thus the more firm the footing you have, the better off you will be able to leap or to prevent yourself from being sucked down a path that may not be beneficial to the company.

Once again, it all goes back to how big is that window, how high is it open, and how long is it going to be open? It tells you how much you can actually get through to effect change. And being in the right window at the right time is the biggest challenge.

How do you know if you should even pursue an opportunity to effect a change? It boils down to can you see the opportunity when it's presented to you? Most business owners are able to process these thoughts and make these decisions without going into an analysis mode or becoming paralyzed by the fear of making a decision. But the only way you can be truly confident that you will identify an event window and know what to do is to practice it.

Think about driving a car on a highway. When you were sixteen years old with your learner's permit, getting out on the road was terrifying. Here comes a semi! How do I shift lanes? Where is my blind spot? There just seemed to be so much going on at once.

Now think about a mature, experienced driver. How much time do you put into the cognitive part of your brain to think about what you're doing while you're driving? You're nowhere near as tentative as you were at sixteen. Small businesses can also have difficulty migrating from the point where they were as a sixteen-year-old driver to the point where they are as a mature driver.

If you apply this analogy to the event window, then here's an opportunity. Can I get in front of this car? Should I pass him in the left lane? Should I move to the right lane? Should I get off at the next exit? Should I hit the brake? Once you become a mature driver you're able to process these thoughts and make these decisions without actually analyzing them and without being paralyzed by fear. But the only way you can gain this confidence is through practice. And the only way you can be truly confident that you will see an event window and know what to do is through practice.

TAKEAWAYS:

1. Critical to the success of managing any opportunity is the ability to make a decision with less than 100% of the information. This takes practice and experience. But most important is the deep understanding of the purpose of your business and why you should take action...or not.

2. Incorporate situational awareness into your everyday practice. You have to understand what you want out of the business, what the business wants out of you, and where you're positioning the business to go.

3. Know your risk tolerance to effect change.

4. Visualize the outcome of the opportunity when it's presented to you. Process these thoughts, and make these decisions without going into analysis paralysis. The only way you can be truly confident that you will see an event window and know what to do is to practice it.

SIX

ENTERING A NEW ECOSYSTEM

(AND HOW TO SURVIVE IN IT)

A lot of assumptions are made about how business models work and how customers interface with businesses and supply chains. Sometimes, what is missed is the bigger context of how businesses interact together as a dynamic, living community. As people interact, and as companies interface, they make connections with each other, which then creates economies.

DEVELOP YOUR STRATEGY TO ENTER INTO THE ECOSYSTEM

When you are inserting yourself into a new industry or creating a new business line, you are introducing yourself as a player in an existing ecosystem. An ecosystem is defined as a community of living organisms, in conjunction with the nonliving components of their environment, interacting as one system. And ecosystems inherently don't like to change. This is certainly demonstrated in the marketplace today. Business ecosystems tend to leverage existing players to keep the ecosystem alive, adhering to standard behaviors that are repeated time after time. And in many cases, the ecosystem will attempt to reject the new business or idea because it perceives it as a threat.

ASSESS WHERE YOUR OPPORTUNITY LIES

Before entry, you need to assess where the opportunity lies to insert your business. If you don't, you can walk into an environment where you're going to be perceived as hostile, or you're going to enter a milieu where you're going to think you're a player in that ecosystem when in fact the system is not going to allow you to be a player.

UNDERSTAND YOUR ROLE

When you want to enter a new ecosystem, you have to find a way that says, "I understand what I'm going into," and then you have to inject yourself into a place that's going to be (1) a safe harbor for you, and (2) a place where you're going to be able to effect change. That change will need to be repeatable and sustainable long enough that the ecosystem will adapt to your presence there. Only then will the members of the network use you on a regular basis, where they come back to you as a repeat customer again and again for transactions or service. At that point, you can build your base.

UNDERSTAND THE ECOSYSTEM ENVIRONMENT

The tendency most of us have is to stay within the same model or use the same network over and over again simply because we're comfortable with it. We know what the transaction cost will be to do business with that individual or customer. In order to be successful in the ecosystem, you must understand its environment. As an example, think about your individual ecosystem. There's a brand of coffee or tea that you always drink. Maybe there's a gas station you always visit. Perhaps there's a store where you always stop to shop. That's an ecosystem because you're going in and you're receiving some goods in response to what you're paying. And you understand it.

Now, if I'm the new person who's coming in from a business standpoint and I want to become part of that ecosystem, perhaps to sell coffee, I have to be aware that there's a Starbucks and a Dunkin' Donuts in the ecosystem where customers already have an existing relationship and are willing to pay the transaction cost to go to that coffee place on a regular basis. For example, I will drive ten miles past the Starbucks just to get to the Dunkin' Donuts, simply because that's my brand and that's what I like.

So when you start putting yourself into that model, you have to consider: "How do I attract new people? What am I going to offer them? How am I going to get them to change their current behavior? And how does that ecosystem then change?"

And remember, not only are you the new coffee shop owner selling coffee outward; you're also the new coffee shop owner buying supplies in that ecosystem. So where you get your supplies will also affect that environment. It becomes a very dynamic interchange among many parties.

Remember, it's not just a business that you're doing business with. It's actual people. And those people are the conduits of how those transactions take place. Even when you go to your supply chain or to your vendors, you're buying from a person, and because you may like that person you might be willing to pay a greater premium for your supplies. You're then going to sell to your customers, who might pay the premium you pass on because they like you and respect your brand.

So an ecosystem becomes this giant spider web of connections of all these different nodes, and as the nodes build up, they become the next level. And then those nodes connect to another set of nodes, and it just continues to expand all the way out. It's important for you to be able to identify where you fit into that web so that you can explain your value proposition at a personal level.

Many times, businesspeople come in with an artificial, ambiguous, non reality-based model where they assume they're going to effect change and don't realize that they are walking into an existing ecosystem where all these players are already connected with one another. They think that their simple appearance into this system is going to effect a change. They don't appreciate the complexity involved in a transaction either on a business-to-business or individual-to-individual basis or how they can provide a product or a service that is going to be sustainable over time.

But there are ways to enter an ecosystem successfully. You have to look at the overall industry and see where there is a high volume of deal-flow. You need to identify where the deal-flow is actually occurring, where the transaction is occurring, and then look at how established that transaction is. Going back to the coffee example, if you're a Dunkin' Donuts fan versus a Starbucks fan and you're now trying to insert yourself into the neighborhood, you need to know how much deal-flow is actually going on and then how much is being invested into that deal-flow from both parties.

Consider the coffee example. Coffee is two to five dollars a cup, but most people don't spend a lot of time thinking about whether they want to go to Starbucks versus Dunkin' Donuts. They just automatically have a routine of buying their coffee where it's convenient. It's not an active thought process to make that decision. So when the coffee shop business considers this, it's going to be very hard for people to transition to somewhere new, to make a change, unless you're willing to give them something else that's going to make you unique and separate you from the other competitors.

I look at this problem first from the aspect of deal-flow: Where is the opportunity? Then I look at what the transaction is that's actually occurring. If it's a cup of coffee, why are they buying coffee there? Is it convenient? Do they like the taste? Are they buying it because the store is right there on the corner? If you could replace that store with your store, would you be able to sustain the model? Looking at it from that context you can say, "That's where the flow is."

Understanding your ecosystem and how close you are to that ecosystem is crucial to being able to make your business a success because you have to be able to leverage that ecosystem. No one really appreciates the magnitude with which it can impact your business. If you have the ability to reach out and touch somebody who can get you in touch with somebody else, that can propel your business further. It is a key component of having a business be successful.

A lack of understanding of the environment can cause you a major problem. It's the fish out of water syndrome. If you believe you're a great white shark but throw yourself into a little pond, you're not going to last very long. Nor will you survive if you're a tiny minnow and you throw yourself into the big blue ocean.

Understanding what that ecosystem is and how it all interrelates gives you a tremendous advantage in how you are going to go after your business and how you are going to go after your customers. Rather than thinking you are going to come in and carve this up into industry segments—an analytical, academic exercise that doesn't take into account that there are actually individuals making the decisions—you have to look at how you can get that individual to change his or her behavior to come and buy your cup of coffee. I think that is one of the biggest differences between what I learned at business school versus the way I see the world really working.

In the ecosystem where STS was first created, we were looking to solve a problem. There were three existing products, and then a fourth product was going to be a new-generation product. When those products were coming to market, there was a limited capacity for them to be used.

Each one of these products was very proprietary, such that they required very specific hardware for the product to work. We ended up bridging the capability among all four products so that they could be interoperable with the same set of hardware. It allowed for the addition of a new feature that would make them portable. Prior to this, the product was mainly a desktop product. We made it transportable. At the time, my father saw an opportunity in the upcoming transition into the advanced digital age. He correctly identified that there was a unique niche that wasn't being met. He came up with the idea and then spent his life savings building the prototype to prove the concept.

The problem was that we were fighting an uphill battle in that the products that existed were made by globally recognized brands at the time. This was in the early 1990s. While we were trying to create a distinctive product that would expand their ability, the truth was that at any given time if those companies had wanted to run us over, they could have. They could have outspent us. They had more money. They had more resources. They could have done whatever they wanted.

But we took the tact of running things very low profile. We were strategic in understanding that we were selling to the federal government where maybe one, two, or three customers at most spent all the money. Even though our first order was for several hundred units and eventually grew to almost two thousand of the products, all of our business was being generated by one individual customer who had the purchasing requirements for the Department of the Army.

We decided to focus our efforts on that and then on the supply chain, which was keeping some of the other large product manufacturers in line with what we were trying to do. Realizing where we were in that ecosystem and that we could get completely run over was a fundamental part of how we defended our space by engaging with them, staying very tightly involved with the customer, and running very low profile to enable us to move quickly until we reached a point where the product was able to be produced and delivered.

To be more specific, the product centered on "landline" phones. (This was years before the mobile phone.) The Department of Defense has a requirement to be able to have point-to-point communications between individuals that cannot be listened to by a third party. It's what they call "secure communications." So you can't just pick up and listen to a conversation, and you can't hack in and do a wiretap to these phones, because they are point-to-point encrypted phone conversations.

At the time, there were three major manufacturers of these phones. In the old days, there was what was called POTS, "plain old telephone service," the phones that people used to have in their houses. But the next digital age of these phones that would increase their capability to send data was on the horizon.

These phones could do point-to-point encryption where the voice sounded like you were talking into an echoing tin can. It sounded very robotic. In the next-generation phone, they were able to clean things up so you could hear voices better. And you could pass more data, so you could actually push faxes through these phones, allowing point-to-point encryption on fax machines. Now you could send a secure fax from one point to another point in the world, and nobody would be able to read it or hack into it or wiretap it.

The problem was that nobody was able to take the phones away from their desk, because they were tied to a specific set of power requirements. What we built was the ability for the phone to be portable. You could stick it in a case, take it anywhere in the world, and plug it into a power supply or plug it into another phone line. Bottom line, you could make that phone portable now and carry it in a briefcase.

However, at the time, none of the manufacturers of those phones felt there was a need to provide this tactical carrying case for their phones. It wasn't part of their product offering. And by itself, one of the three main manufacturers didn't see adequate justification for it.

But if you put all three phones together, along with the next generation, a total of four phones, you had a market because you could put any one of those four phones in the briefcase. If you looked at it as a narrow segment and said, "I'm buying one phone, one case," it didn't make sense. But if I have one case and multiple phones, it did make sense. The customer became interested because he didn't have to buy a separate case for each phone. The ability to make them transportable was another key feature. So that was a niche at the time.

That's what started the company off, that specific opportunity. And because my dad had already worked in the industry and for the army, he had been able to observe the entire ecosystem. He knew who the key players were, which ones were willing to play, which ones were not willing to play, which ones were defensive, and which ones were territorial. We were intimately involved with how the ecosystem worked at the time. We knew where all the pressure points were to get things to move forward.

That, of course, is looking at it in hindsight. We walked into the ecosystem like most small businesses do, with more of a stumble than a walk. We did not think through the process of entering the ecosystem, how it worked, and the supply and demand transaction or the deal-flow. Like most small businesses, out of sheer luck and ignorance we said, "I have an idea. Let's go sell this product," and we did. Over time, the analogy to an ecosystem became more relevant to me. It made more sense about how it all works and where it all comes together.

If we had gone back to the business school model and said, "We're going to slice this up by market segment, and we're going to figure out who the customer is. We're going to get the price point, and we're going to sell it." It wouldn't have worked. We would have been trying to hit some demographic that didn't exist.

And that's how over the last ten years we've been successful. We've been able to evaluate internally what do we do well and what our customers really appreciate and then leverage that into another ecosystem. We can look at a client, look at their requirements and their needs, and figure out how we can provide value to them so that they will be willing to do business with us and thus develop new streams of revenue. We've been able to do that consistently, year over year, for the last twenty years.

But remember what I said: the ecosystem is going to try and expel you. In our case there was a lack of participation by the existing incumbent companies that were already in the market space. The product manufacturers didn't have any desire to support us, because it didn't increase the sales of their phones. While they weren't necessarily trying to expel us, they weren't trying to help us either. Their sales were based on their phones, not on our cases, so they had no vested interest in supporting us. So how do you get someone to pay attention to you who doesn't have any need to? That was one big challenge for us.

And then there were other competitors. Once we had started getting some traction and moved from the initial prototypes to an order that was almost 1,600 units, all of a sudden there were a lot of people paying attention to us. It's a lot of money, especially when you think about rolling it out on an even larger scale.

The lesson here is to understand where you fit in the marketplace and how you fit in your own ecosystem. This is crucial. It makes it much easier for you, as an individual company or as an individual professional, to navigate what you're trying to accomplish. It's not necessarily always what's right in front of you that is making the organization or the business work.

Becoming aware of what's happening around you, who's making what decisions, how they are being made, why they are made, and who the other players are in the decisions (the winners, the losers, the stakeholders) is important. You start finding out who the people are who make the decisions that influence the way an organization goes, one way or the other. And for you to understand that is critical.

Simply because you have a great product doesn't mean it will sell itself. You have to be able to understand the organizational level of how it's constructed, what it does, how it fits into the marketplace, and where the industry will allow it to go. The way you establish yourself is by providing an honest, quality product to the customer. It's much easier to make a sale or get someone to include you in their network when they respect you as an individual. People do business with people. It doesn't matter whether you're selling a product, a service, or an idea. The same principles still apply. You need to be well connected and well networked in your ecosystem as a professional, a leader, and a new person in an organization. The more you work on building that network and ecosystem and understand how the world around you works and how transactions occur, the more opportunity you will have to make yourself meaningful to them.

And when I say networking, I'm not talking about going out and meeting somebody and exchanging business cards. That's not networking, that's socializing. You need to establish the network so that people you meet understand who you are and what your relevance is to them.

It's a continual, ongoing process to stay engaged on a daily basis or a weekly basis so that when those customers have a need you can meet, they will actually turn to you. This goes back to what we talked about before: the art of selling.

You may build the next greatest mousetrap or sell the next best brand of coffee, but if you're not aware of who needs to see it, who needs to sample it, who needs to potentially do a transaction with you, it will go nowhere.

From there you need to understand where the people are within the organization that you need to interface with and work with in order to make what you want to have happen actually happen, whether it's to buy your product, to believe in your idea, or to get you promoted.

The only way you can do this is to stay aware of your ecosystem at all times and keep your head up and look at the bigger context of all that surrounds you. You need to see where the opportunities lie with certain people and where those people play a role in their own organization, in their own sphere of influences.

TAKEAWAYS:

1. Understanding your role in your ecosystem and how you can best leverage the relationships that you foster within the ecosystem is crucial to a successful business.

2. Simply because you have a great product doesn't mean it will sell itself. You have to be able to understand the organizational level of how it's constructed, what it does, how it fits into the marketplace, and where the industry will allow it to go.

SEVEN

NEVER TURN DOWN A MEETING

(CAST A WIDE NET)

One of the things I always tell my staff is, "Never turn down a meeting." This is especially true if there's the potential for an introduction or a longer term business opportunity. This obviously can't be a hard and fast rule, since no one can take meetings all day long, or no work would ever get accomplished. However, within reason and whenever able, you need to be able to present yourself at every opportunity you get.

PUT YOURSELF OUT THERE

And when I say "meeting," I'm not just talking about a business meeting where you walk in, sit down with an agenda, and take notes. I'm not talking about an office call where you sit across the table from a new potential client or a new supplier or a new vendor. I'm talking about anything from an opening for a meeting that came out of attending a birthday party for a coworker to an invitation to meet with a new business that just opened its doors. By presenting yourself and putting yourself out there when the target of opportunity arises, you continue to build your visibility in the environment around you, and you never know where that might lead you.

There are so many businesspeople, and I've witnessed this frequently, who act as if they don't have the time or it's too much effort for them to commit to a meeting. They are so busy with their daily business that they lose sight of the fact that whatever they are working on today is going to end. This "heads-down" mentality will potentially lead to missed opportunities as well as lack of awareness of what is going on around you. You'll never be able to reach out quickly enough when an opportunity or event window opens, and you'll be at a massive disadvantage compared to all who are already plugged in.

In most careers, 80 percent of the struggle is just showing up to work on time and doing what you're asked to do. If you do that, just show up when you're supposed to, dress in the appropriate manner, and deliver what you're asked to deliver, I can promise you're going to have a successful career. But if you're looking to dial it up and achieve that next level of success, you need to start identifying how you're going to differentiate yourself from everyone else.

One of the best ways you can do that is to make yourself relatable when you have the chance to meet a new contact. Maybe that contact is a new business in your office building. Don't hesitate to go, because you might strike up a conversation with someone you didn't know before, and then the next thing you know you may find a new opportunity or meet a new vendor that's going to save you 50 percent over cost on business you're currently doing. Don't become so enamored with doing what you're doing right now that you don't venture out. I can tell you that it was flexibility and the ability to jump faster than everybody else that got STS recognized as a motivated team.

An example of this recently happened to me. I requested a meeting with a gentleman in Charleston, South Carolina. He agreed, and I went down to see him. We stayed engaged, and because I was responsive to meet him within his time frame, he contacted me again and said, "I've got a contract opportunity coming up. I might be able to fit you guys in. It'll be probably about forty to fifty people if you get the work." Forty to fifty people is a lot of money. But getting that contract opportunity had nothing to do with market segments and customers and all the other traditional business development and customer strategies that you learn in MBA programs. It was about the fact that when he said he was available to meet, I presented myself as quickly as I possibly could. I went to Charleston faster and quicker than anyone else. If I said I'd do it by 5:00, I delivered at 4:00. If he said he wanted a meeting tomorrow, I'd be sitting in front of his office fifteen minutes prior to the meeting. Not turning down a meeting or a phone call and always being willing to engage, combined with the awareness of being able to move when you see the opportunity, gets you out in front faster than everybody else. And really, when you think about it, it's not that big of a time commitment nor does it create utter chaos in your schedule.

You simply don't turn the meeting down, and the next thing you know, that meeting spins into another meeting, and then you maintain a positive rapport with this person and go forward.

When I take a meeting with somebody, regardless of what the meeting may be, I look at how it is going to make us more effective and more efficient. How is this interaction going to bring more "good revenue" to STS? Are we doing something of importance to meet our mission and our value statement? We're not going to go out and do some random job simply because it's awarded to us. It's got to be something that's going to produce value to the corporation, which increases our prestige and increases our opportunities down the line.

IT'S A SMALL WORLD AFTER ALL

There is that closeness factor once you start realizing that the world is very small. When you start meeting people, you have to remain very conscious of the fact that you may be calling on this person again in two months or two years, and you may need that person as a business relationship or a business contact to propel your business into the next strata. Whether it's growth, or the penetration of a new market, or even if you're just looking for advice and assistance, or a partnership with another company to spin out a new business line, you have to be very conscious of the smallness of the ecosystem.

Whether in small towns or large cities, there is a very tight ecosystem of people, a network of contacts, who are in your space and know what's going on. If you're able to stay on top of that, you will be able to draw upon that system when you need to do so. If you go into this as just a chance to schmooze, walking around and shaking everybody's hand, you're wasting your time. People will see right through that. It's that transparent.

There is a time and a place for socializing like that, but if you're trying to drive your business, that's not what you want to spend your time doing. You want to be the company that's going to deliver true value. You want to be the person who is sincere and empathetic. You want to listen to the person across from you and understand what they're telling you and engage them as an active listener. You want to understand what their problem is and how you can help them become more effective. This, in the end, is also going to help *you* because it will build trust. That's a relationship factor that you can leverage.

I try to do that not just with STS stakeholders but also with competitors, because today's competitor could be tomorrow's partner. You can't allow today's business decision to impact your future reputation with anybody.

It's okay to look someone square in the eye and tell them you can't do business with them on this one because it isn't in your own business's self-interest. What you want to make sure to add is: "While I can't bring you on this time, I'd like to keep the doors open, so let's continue to communicate and move forward." Then you can use that as your own leverage point later because you never know when you might be able to tap that person. But if you're never willing to open up the door and have a meeting and conversation, you're never going to be granted that opportunity when you need to call on someone in the future.

When you have a meeting, you're going to do research first. You're going to figure out who your customer is, especially if it's a client-facing meeting. We've all heard the tips like, "Try to find out what their interests are, search on LinkedIn or Facebook. Start figuring out who they are so you can create some sort of synergy." Or "When you are seated in their office, scan their workplace and look for something in their office that you can start a conversation around. For example, if they have pictures of their kids playing baseball, you can jump into a baseball conversation."

You know what? Those are all great small hooks, but that's all they are, hooks. If you're not sincerely engaged with somebody, and you can't make that connection, the meeting will fall apart and quickly become very awkward. The other person will realize it's just an amateurish, inadequate, and uncomfortable conversation. But if you're truly engaged, you'll never be considered to be making small talk, because you're truly interested in what somebody else is saying.

IF PEOPLE LIKE YOU, THEY'LL LISTEN TO YOU

I do think there's a complete lack of attention to the art of active engagement and listening in conversation. It has become less about trying to connect with the individual and more about trying to broadcast your ideas to the masses, being able to extract what their idea was to then reference it to somebody else. It's retweeting somebody saying, "Did you see this?" That becomes so superficial within itself that you're not truly relevant. Why? Because now they can just bypass you to go directly to that person's Twitter feed and get the same information. Who needs you? All you're doing is broadcasting stuff. This is not how you connect in business. In business it's about people and value proposition, and you have to focus on that side of it. So when you take meetings, you have to commit to them. You need to create an environment or a discussion where they will walk away with the opinion that you are sincerely committed and that there is value in taking the time to meet with you. You want them to remember the person, not the email address and not the Twitter feed. I think that's a challenge.

The concept of "social proximity" is another often-touted business principle. Social proximity dictates that the closer you are connected to a leader or a manager or an executive determines your power and your ability to influence. But from a leadership perspective, your goal is to make connections with enough people that your ideas and thoughts and your values resonate. And then it perpetuates itself. However, you will never resonate with everyone.

But you *can* engage effectively with your vendors and your suppliers and your employees and your partner companies and even your competitors. You have to stay engaged. You never know when you are going to need them, and to separate yourself and circle 'round the wagons in a very close group prevents you from being agile and flexible and transparent when the market demands because you are too insular. If you spend all your time talking to the same three people, that business avenue is a dead end, because it has already been exhausted. You wasted time and money, and that's painful, especially when you're a small business and you don't have a lot of money to spend.

IF PEOPLE TRUST YOU, THEY'LL WORK WITH YOU

Let's also consider the concept of "regulated competition." Regulated competition refers to a small group that competes for a small set of clients. In the case of STS, we compete within the government and the Department of Defense market space for business. We know what the clients' budgets are because they are published annually. There's a lot of competition for these contracts out there, and when we do proposal work, we start ghosting what the other team may propose. Ghosting involves placing yourself in your competitor's mind-set to develop strategies to counter their approach. For instance, we ghost that they're going to disclose that they are the low-cost leader or that they're going to argue they are the most technically qualified company because they have experts who are competent above and beyond everybody else.

As part of the process, you begin to understand that if you're going to continue competing with this group of businesses, this is what they are going to say. This is how they are going to go after the proposals. That helps you because you can start determining what your brand is. This is what you're going to go after. It makes no sense for me to go after a contract where they are really looking for low bargain-basement pricing if I'm a mid-size company that has professional salaries and all my employees are graduate school level and above, because I'm not going to win that bargain-basement contract with those qualifications.

When you ghost your competition, you can get a good feel for how companies are looking at business opportunities and what customers they are targeting. If you do this enough you can start to build a great understanding of who your competition is; how they will go after clients; and what the client's are actually interested in. By developing a detailed understanding of your competition and the clients, you gain a much greater understanding of your ability to address needs in a way that your competition does not. It does not matter what the business is or who the client is. What matters is that you develop an intimate understanding of the needs you are trying to address. Once you focus in on that you can deliver the message in a way that honest and direct to the client that will resonate with them and builds trust. Earning trust is the key to many things in life and especially in business.

In any market, it's fairly easy to find out who your competition is. You quickly become aware of who you are going to compete against on a regular basis. All you need to do is ask. You just have to have the guts to stand in front of somebody and say, "Why didn't I get the business?" And "What can I do next time to improve my position to get the business?" It's the same set of circumstances, the same set of challenges. In the end, it's just you versus all these other businesses that are going after your business because so many companies can enter the market and exit the market so quickly.

TAKEAWAYS:

1. Don't get so caught up in the details that you miss an opportunity.

2. Listen. Understand. Actively engage.

3. What is your value proposition? Create and effectively deliver the message of your value proposition.

EIGHT

IT'S NOT JUST ABOUT YOU ANYMORE

(NOW YOU'RE A SUCCESS)

All successful companies evolve over time, making it difficult to maintain the original culture. Additionally, company leaders may no longer have that adrenaline rush and intensity that was so palpable in the early days of development.

Once you get past that nascent stage of developing your company and you get past the massive growth stage, which is from zero dollars to your first $100,000 or $1 million or $10 million, then the company starts becoming its own ongoing concern, its own living self, and there are pieces and parts around everywhere. At that point, it's hard to maintain the intimate relationship that existed amid the intensity of the start-up phase. I think that's a healthy thing for most companies because you can't burn the candle at both ends for an extended period of time without burning yourself out or without the company imploding or running out of money or running out of time and energy. You just can't do that. So making that transition from where everything was super intense, where you put in 110 percent effort working crazy hours just trying to make it, to something that's a little bit more stable and manageable is a good thing. But a lot of people have a problem with transitioning from putting in sixty, seventy, eighty hours a week or more, which is a normal workweek for a start-up or an entrepreneur.

Then you have to look at your forty-hour-a-week employees and be careful not to cast judgment or make an opinion about them because they are only putting in forty hours a week. It doesn't mean they're less able to contribute to your organization. It doesn't mean their contribution isn't as important. I work crazy hours because I am trying to do ten different jobs at the same time. If I only had to do one job, could I do it for forty hours a week? Well, then I shouldn't hold it against somebody if they're working forty hours a week and doing the job.

It's really hard to let that go when you're wired a certain way. It's survival for you, a high locus of self-control where you're defining your own world and relationships with the environment. If you make a decision you can make it happen.

MANAGING SUCCESSFUL PEOPLE

If you're successful, eventually you will bring other people in who have a different way of doing business. It's healthy to have those people around you because it provides a different perspective or different frame of reference about how you should perceive the world. Although the business is your life and you're trying to grow your business, which then pays for your house and your mortgage and everything else, you can't necessarily inflict that or impose that point of view on somebody else. So you need to keep a healthy balance and make sure you understand their point of view as opposed to just your own point of view.

Most employees don't stop to think that the business is tied to their reputation. But it is a reflection of your own personality or your own self-worth, and you should value your reputation and your position in your industry. Therefore, when others reflect that something is not a big deal, you as an owner react that it *is* a big deal. In fact, it's a *huge* deal. You see it as a black mark against your name, which is also against your company. As an owner, it can be difficult to balance and to convince your team that failing to deliver to the company's customers (internal or external) impacts their own personal and professional reputation.

One of the things I learned when I was in the fire department managing a volunteer organization (we had 150-200 members at any given time) was that I was asking people to do something for free. They were giving up their weekends. They were giving up their holidays. They were giving up their nights. We used to mandate that everybody had to put in a minimum of twelve hours in a shift per week. You would get assigned to a given day or to a night, and you would sleep over on whatever night of the week that was. It could be a Friday night, a Tuesday night, or a Saturday day, whatever you were assigned.

This was a huge wake-up call to me, and it was a big eye-opener to me as well. Imagine that every person in this organization is working for free and sacrificing part of their life for some sort of reward they are getting out of volunteering to the organization. But it wasn't all the same reward for everyone. The eighteen-year-old full of adrenaline had just seen a movie on TV and wanted to be a hero. That's one person. The forty-year-old just hit his midlife crisis and was trying to get his youth back. That's a different person. The older guy just wanted to be out of the house. Someone else wanted to do it for social reasons. Others wanted to feel like they were giving to the greater good of the community. Every single member had a different motivation, all of which were equally important to the organization.

The challenge came in when you had to look at these different types of personalities and figure out how to manage them and to encourage and engage them. What do you do, how do you reward them, how do you get them to be as productive as they can be? You have to take what you can and contribute to the organization because it's all of significant value. It took me a longer time to pull that lesson from the volunteer side to the corporate side. Before this I just thought that every employee was out there just to try and make money. They brought us in revenue and helped make us a success, and we gave them a paycheck in return. Now I understood for the first time that the paycheck had very little to do with their motivation.

You have to understand each individual's motivation for showing up to work every day, and manage and encourage them in a way that they're getting a return for what they're contributing, what they're sacrificing out of their own life to come to the organization. Yes, you pay them, but to have them truly contribute, they need to be able to come to the table with their own points of view. It's much different when you're a start-up, where the environment can be very intense. But once you get to that mature state of development with your company, you need a mix of people and perspectives to balance out an organization and to make you healthy.

MANAGING COMPANY GROWTH

I would say there are four major stages of a company's growth span. There's the start-up/initial phase, then comes the rapid growth phase, followed by the mature/plateau phase, and finally a decline and smoldering phase. Granted, at any given time there are going to be multiple contributing factors to these stages. You have to have the passion, the motivation, the energy to start up a business, but you also have to have the financial resources to be able to afford it. There is human capital that comes with the people able to do the work, and you also have to have the idea. You need to have all those pieces work together at the same time to really get something growing and growing well.

Start-Up Phase

This is the beginning phase of all businesses and can last for a very short period, or you may never get out of it. You have already thought of the business idea and the business model for you to achieve your goals. Funding the business is the biggest concern. Where the next cash infusion is going to come from is the greatest stress you will have. Whether it comes from one or all of the three Fs (family, friends, and fools) or you get backing from some private source of funding such as an early-stage angel investor or some private institution, this is still a time of incredible excitement and stress.

During this time you are usually bootstrapping it, doing everything you possibly can to make the business work, and working incredibly long hours, giving up family or personal time just to get a chance to last one more month or week. There were a number of times that I could not take a paycheck during this phase for our company.

This is also the time you end up finding your first "real" customer. Real in the sense that you are not getting favors from friends to help kickstart the business. When you close on your first deal from a cold lead, meaning you had no previous awareness of the opportunity or customer, it is an absolutely exhilarating feeling.

Businesses also begin to experiment with new business models, delivery methods, and targeted customers. Based on my experience, by the time you move out of the start-up phase, the business model will look very different from what you thought at the outset.

This is also the time in a business where the foundation of the culture and the beliefs of the company take hold. It is during the times of struggle and stress that you begin to develop the work ethic and confidence in yourself and your business. As a business owner and leader I think you appreciate how hard it can be when you have to struggle to make it work.

Some of the businesses that I have seen with the most dysfunction and the most trouble are those that have too easy a go at business in the start-up phase. Too much, too soon can be a big challenge.

If you have never felt adversity, you fail to appreciate the guts and sacrifice it takes when things truly get hard.

Growth Phase

Coming out of a start-up phase, all businesses enter a grow phase. The growth could be rapid, it could be controlled, or it could be incremental at best. During the growth phase, the business begins to mature and develops into an ongoing business concern, meaning that you are not truly carrying the business day to day.

Managing growth is one of the greatest times for a business—you get more customers and more deals, and you are earning money. However, it could be also one of the most challenging times. During the start-up phase, everything is new. You had no idea what you were truly walking into. So every day was an adventure, everything was a new challenge.

In the growth phase, those challenges become real work. As you grow, you earn a lot more responsibilities. Whether it is hiring your first round of employees outside the initial core group, getting a loan from a bank to make payroll, or getting your first really big deal, it is only then that you begin to learn of all the rules, regulations, processes, and so on.

When you start to grow, the business really begins to take shape. In the start-up phase the business is a passion; during the growth phase it becomes a job. Before, you could be involved in almost everything, but when you grow you simply cannot. So hiring the right people at the right time becomes your greatest challenge.

One of the biggest risks is transitioning away from the founder mentality of running the business and finding the right people to manage the growth. There are a lot of different levels of managing a business, and the people that are good managing a small business typically do not do as well when the business gets large.

The same is true for the inverse. A lot of people coming from a large business have no idea what it takes to grow a successful small business. They can be really good, competent people, but in the wrong business they could be a disaster.

Plateau

During this phase, running the business moves from a job to a profession, meaning that you are now becoming an expert at running the business. You become highly attuned to running the business and manage incremental business process improvement to maximize effectiveness and efficiencies.

This can be a great time for any business. You have customers and you are making money. So you finally get to enjoy the fruits of all the hard work and sacrifice.

However, the plateau phase of any business is often the most dangerous. During the plateau phase, the business model and the ideas can begin to stagnate. Your competition starts to eat away at your customers and take them away.

After exiting the growth phase, people become overconfident and comfortable. Simply because there is a success in the growth of a business does not mean it will continue. A lot of people are reluctant to reinvest or reinvent themselves—it would mean going back to where they struggled so hard to get out of in the start-up phase. The larger a business becomes, the harder it is to effect a wholesale change to react to market conditions or new impacts to your ecosystem.

One of the biggest risks in this phase is the lack of growth or lack of emphasis on pushing forward for more business. As you grow, there is a risk of complacency and a risk of forgetting the survival skills learned in earlier phases. If you cannot instill survival skills or the desire to succeed, to continue the business the only real alternative is to scale up the resources. But this is challenging for everyone in the business—you cannot just throw money and people at the problem and think it will make a difference.

Too much time in a plateau will inevitably result in a business losing its ability to continue to be successful. The hardest part here is that you cannot predict it—you will only realize it after it is too late, and you have started into the next phase—decline.

Decline

We've done it countless times when the company was going through its cycle: the idea was there and the money was there, but we didn't make the right decision at the right time. There were times when we were entering that smoldering phase where we were still putting off a little bit of heat, but there was no real growth. There was no new massive energy, and then all of a sudden at the right time and place, we saw the opportunity and either took the risk and jumped into something that we normally wouldn't have jumped into, or we just poured gasoline on the fire at the right time and it was enough to get the ideas and the motivations going again.

I remember at one point we had just been notified that we'd lost our biggest contract. It was devastating. It was a program that we'd identified ourselves with as our brand. We were great at the work, and the customer liked us. Unfortunately, a new company that had no real experience underbid us. It took us by surprise—the winds were definitely taken out of our sails. We were almost at a dead stop, with only a few long-shot opportunities that were still months out. Weeks and then months went by. We were within days of having to shut down the program, with no new prospects, when a call came out of the blue that we won one of the programs we'd bid on as a subcontractor. We'd bid it almost a year before and did not even know if we had a chance to win. Overnight, we went from having to cut the staff by ten people to having to ramp up an additional twenty-five people in less than thirty days.

Another example of this centers around one of the products that we built for the US Army. It was a small mobile surveillance kit. It was modular, easy to use, and low cost—a great product. However, we could never get it to take off on a large scale. Time and time again, we would get significant interest from a group of clients who would buy only a small quantity and only if we made some changes. We would tweak the product to meet their needs and then nothing—no follow-up orders. Months would go by and then we would receive another small order from a different customer. In the meantime, we had to reprioritize the team to focus on products that had more potential. Then we finally hit the right customer, had the resources and experience, and had an opportunity that grew out of only an ember to a fully funded program. Several million dollars in product sales later, we are thankful that we tended to that effort. Many times, the ember could have gone out, but by paying enough attention to keep it alive, we were able to bring it roaring back in what turned out to be a great business plan.

But again, what is crucial here is that when you mature as a company, you also need to mature as a person and look for those types of personalities that will contribute to the organization. You need to look for personality and potential in your employees. My preference is to employ a person with a less-than-stellar resume with whom I can resonate and who has the energy to contribute to the job we're hiring for. I care less about their pedigree or the degrees they hold or what they did on their resume, because, at the end of the day, as a small business when you start hiring key personnel, it's more about what they are going to bring to the table. How are they going to make you more effective? How are they going to make you more efficient? How are they going to help you do this cheaper, faster, and better than what you did yesterday? A resume gives me some evidence of that, but it's a piece of paper that somebody can make look any way they want it to. They can enhance it, focus on the good parts, and leave out the bad parts.

For example, recently I was looking to hire someone to perform a specific function inside the company. I went through the resumes on my desk and found a highly qualified, competent candidate. His resume was a progression—every two or three years a new job, a new title, a master's degree, working on a Ph.D., always moving forward. I brought him in for an interview and talked to him at length. It was a perfect interview. He appeared to be a perfect candidate for the job.

The first day he was in the office, I realized it was not going to work out. He had worked in large businesses his entire career. When he sat down in a small business, he found he was working without a safety net. He was on the project for three months when he came back to me with a budget and a plan. He said he would need a year to complete the project, which was reasonable. He then added that he would need seventeen new employees to execute it.

Let me repeat, he was asking me to hire seventeen new workers to complete a project that he was an expert on. The seventeen employees were going to create a process that the company currently had six people working on—he was looking to hire seventeen people to manage the six people who were actually doing the work. I asked him what part of that equation he didn't get.

His reply was that this was what he needed to get the job done and that this was how he had done it at all the previous companies he had worked at. The absurdity was lost on him.

That was a big eye-opener for me. Now when I hire, I still do a review of the candidate's resume. Do they look like someone I would want to work with? When they come in for an interview, however, I don't even look at the resume, because I'm trying to evaluate the potential of the candidate. Anybody can be trained to do a job, but if that person doesn't have the right mind-set, if they won't fit into the company culture, forget it. It just won't work. Again, something you learn through experience.

Another caution when hiring: you also don't want to hire a replica of yourself. You want to find someone who will come in and contribute to the organization. Do you have a personal connection with them? Can you see where they're trying to go and what they will be able to bring to the table? Some of the greatest contributors I've hired for the company have been people you would not have expected. They're not the ones about whom you would say, "This one's a rock star." But if you can make a personal connection with the hire, then the potential for them to contribute just blossoms. Those are the people you really want to keep a lookout for and not necessarily get enamored with someone's stellar resume.

Also keep in mind that the people you start out with are not necessarily the people you will need ten years down the road, despite the fact that they helped make the company a success. The truth is that the people who helped start it up are not necessarily the people who will be good at running the organization. So if you are a small organization of ten people, it's a very different game than running an organization of a thousand people. Just because you're a great leader and manager of ten people does not mean you will be a great leader and manager of a thousand people. That's a hard thing to learn. You assume that the ten employees who started the company will always be the senior executive staff, but it's not necessarily so. Sometimes it works, sometimes it doesn't.

This doesn't mean you have to let them go. My point of view is to continue to build strength around them. When you are small, everyone is working very hard, and you often don't see what's fallen through the cracks. But as you get larger as a company, the cracks become much more significant because you can't just run around and pick everything up when the organization becomes more spread out.

So the best plan is to hire people that you trust and respect and then build around them. Provide them with the supportive infrastructure to make them successful. Not everybody is going to be able to continue to progress with the company as it grows over time. Some people have personal and professional limitations that make them unable to contribute. Maybe they have a family issue they have to deal with. Maybe their significant other or spouse has to move for work. Whatever the case, they may be unable to contribute the way you need them to contribute at the time. It doesn't mean they're not of value to the organization anymore. You just need to determine how to best utilize them. You need to determine what they *are* able to contribute. Like I said, it's a hard thing to do when you start looking at your senior employees. You remember and appreciate all that they did for you in the last five or ten years, but you still need to go out and bring in a new person from outside who will end up being their peer. That's a tough decision to make, but sometimes it's what is in the best interest of the company.

There are other ways you can compensate or reward senior workers for their contributions. You can bonus them, or you can give them stock options. But you need to understand that if you want the company to grow, there will be times when you have to make difficult decisions. There will be points when you have to recognize that this is no longer the best person for the position and that you need to get someone else to come in and do that job. It can be tough at times, but at STS, we just continue work with these employees and find out how they will continue to contribute professionally and personally.

As our organization grew larger and larger, we became hyper-focused on the "closer" position. Initially I was a closer on a lot of the business, but then what happened is that the customer expected me to always be there, and thus by default I became part of the customer's expectations—I was trapped with the customer always wanting personal attention from me. Not their fault, as I was the one who set the initial customer expectation. But what I found was that, as the company grew, the business demanded more of my time, so what I had to do was eventually transition out and bring in other people.

That's a hard thing to do because now you're not there making decisions for the customers who are actually paying the bills for the company. You can't clone yourself, so you need to empower others to get out there and make decisions in the best interest of the organization. They have to understand what your business intent is, what your goals are, and what your vision means, so they can adapt that to the customer's requirements. These employees become the most essential people in the company.

In the typical business school model, you would sit down with a focus group. You would carve up the market and identify a target and then go off and pitch the corporate line. It's a more academic approach: "This is what the market is missing. This is where we're going to position a product. This is what we're going to sell. This is who we're going to sell to. And this is how it's going to be sold." It's almost formulaic, as opposed to orienting it the other way around. When you are driving it as an entrepreneur start-up, your ideas resonate with a specific set of clients and customers. As the company scales and you get bigger, you can't be the person who's the touch-point with all of your clients. You just can't. It's one thing if you have one, two, or maybe two dozen clients. You could rush around from point to point to talk to them. But as your company grows to hundreds of clients, you may not be able to do that anymore. That's why you need key people who understand your vision.

Many believe that working in your own business, being the owner must be great. "It's so awesome to be your own boss." I just sit there and shake my head at that statement. Yes, it's fun when you first start up and you're on your own and you can decide today's going to be casual day and you're going to wear flip-flops. Eventually, as the organization gets bigger, the reality is that you're the boss of no one and everybody else is your boss because they all are telling you what to do.

You have to pay the bills or you have to talk to the client or you have to talk to your lawyer or talk to your accountant about one issue or another. They're all giving you information and you're the *one* who has to make a decision. You are making the decision that results in action, and you have to follow through on that action. Everyone thinks that as the boss you've climbed to the top of the pyramid and that you're standing at the top looking down at everyone else. I see it the other way around. My perspective is that you've climbed to the top of the pyramid, and at the end of the day it flips upside down on you, and you're actually standing at the bottom of the pyramid balancing the entire pyramid in the palm of your hand.

It's like balancing a broomstick on your finger where you're constantly moving, trying to keep everything balanced and in line. Sometimes it tips one way, and sometimes it tips the other way. Sometimes you only have to move your hand, and sometimes you have to run your entire body over there to keep everything from falling. When you're the owner and you get bigger and you have forward-facing people who are interfacing with vendors or customers or employees themselves, you're relying on them to get things done to carry forward the collective vision and mission of the organization. What ends up happening is that they become the boss of you because you need them to be able to make the work happen. If you don't have them, the work's not going to happen and you can't fill it by yourself.

There is a healthy balance where it's great to be the boss and be able to make all these decisions, but the reality is that if no one's going to listen to you or you don't have the people to do the work that you need to get done, you're really not the boss of anything. So you're constantly flipping back and forth on how you manage employees to get them to do what you need them to do. At the same time, you have to listen to what they're telling you and be responsive to what they're asking of you. It doesn't matter where they are in the organization, whether it's supply chain, employees, customers, other peers, or other peer companies. You're constantly being tugged in a thousand different directions because it's not just about you anymore.

This is when it is key to get back to the original understanding of what the ideal state of what you are trying achieve is. You must have the courage to look inward and question whether what you have created is still in line with the plans that you originally laid out. Or have your goals evolved, and do they match what you want now? A friend of mine had this very problem. When he started his business, he had a very clear plan of wanting to be a lean company of only fifteen to twenty very high-performing people that could do a lot of creative things. A victim of his own success, he grew the company to over three hundred people and was doing great. But the business model he was serving was service oriented, which means he had people spread around at customer sites providing administrative and technical support. So his vision of being a technical solution provider morphed into being a staffing agency. Although a successful one, it still was not his passion.

One day at a conference I caught up with him, and he said he was considering getting out of the company and going back to his original plans of a smaller group of people who were intimately involved with the customer. You see, as he grew, the demand of running the business every day had taken out the creativity and passion of solving highly complex, technical problems. Now he was dealing with political infighting among the executives, employee issues, and working with the banks for finances and contracting.

His view of success had changed. When he started, his passion was to help customers directly and be involved. Now at the head of a large business, most of his time was taken with process and bureaucracy. When we talked through it all, he could have made a little less money but been much happier.

TAKEAWAYS:

1. Human capital is the soul and the future of your organization. You must understand each individual's motivation for showing up to work every day and manage them such that they receive a return for their contribution.

2. You can't clone yourself! Take time to identify and groom the next generation in your company. Have the courage to empower and delegate staff to make decisions in the best interest of the organization.

NINE

IN THE END

(IT TAKES GUTS)

If I were to sum up what I've talked about, the stories that I've tried to relay, and some of the experiences I've conveyed through the previous chapters, the crux of it would be that starting up a business takes a lot of guts. It has been said, "No guts, no glory," but the truth is it takes a lot of guts for a little glory. It requires a lot of commitment, a lot of sacrifice, and a lot of long, long, long hours to make a company successful. It means giving up some of your personal time that you could have spent doing something else. Being an entrepreneur is not for the weak at heart, but I can tell you it's worth it.

Yes, it's a huge challenge, but the rewards are worth the risks. You must understand from the outset that the journey is part of the reward. You can't look on your undertaking as a get-rich-quick scheme. You can't be enamored with the idea of being your own boss. Starting a business is not about being in charge and making tons of money. There are very few businesses that actually make a huge windfall as a start-up business. It's more of a choice of what you want to do with your life. There will be a lot of naysayers along the way, from your bank that will deny you credit, to customers who will slam the door in your face, to your network of friends and family who will look at you as if you were crazy. "Why are you going to go do this?

Why are you putting yourself through all the stress? You could go work for somebody else and have no stress."

They're not wrong. It is a difficult thing to do, but it is also probably the most rewarding thing you could do. There's nothing like walking into your own office for the very first time or when a customer calls you and tells you they're awarding you the contract. You validate all of the long days and longer nights and skipped vacations and missed holidays with these little nuggets that make you realize that it's been a successful journey. Then you sleep for a second, and it starts all over again. But you have to understand going into it that not everyone will end up a Bill Gates or a Steve Jobs or a Mark Zuckerberg. If that's your goal in starting a business, then you're doing it for the wrong reason. Is it possible? Absolutely it's possible. Never give up that dream if that's what your dream is, but the reality is it's a long shot, and it's going to take a lot of hard work to get there if you do make it.

At the end of the day, starting a business has to be something that you are gauging your own success at. You have to determine whether or not what you are going to sacrifice is going to be worth it to you because it does come with a cost. I'm not a big fan of the whole work-life balance hype. Work-life balance is meaningless to me. It's an artificial term. Work and life are interdependent. You can't balance the two, and *your* balance would not be *my* balance, nor should it be.

So if you want that excitement and that challenge, you need to go into the enterprise with your eyes wide open and realize that it's going to be a lot of *hard work*. There are going to be a lot of *long nights*. There are going to be a lot of people who tell you *no*, and there are going to be moments when you are in complete, utter *despair* because you lost a contract or a customer or you don't know how you're going to pay the bills. You never know what's going to happen next, and then all of a sudden it will be the greatest day of your life because you snared a new contract. You have new opportunities. You're getting to hire new people.

I don't think I would have ever had the opportunity to do the things that I have done today if I had gone down another path. I think I would probably have been moderately successful in somebody else's business where I could contribute to the organization. I probably would have done okay financially. I probably would have been fine professionally. Would I have been satisfied? Who knows? But I can say I probably wouldn't have traveled the world. I wouldn't have met all the people I have met. I wouldn't have gone to all the places I've gone. My path has been such a fulfilling experience that anything else I could have done, from a financial standpoint or from a professional standpoint, pales in comparison to the personal experiences that I've had.

As soon as you get out of college or out of high school and are working your first job, you start making new friends. You start dating your significant other, you get married, you have kids, you buy a house, and the next thing you know life has passed you by. It goes back to the concept of the event window. People have a hard time letting go and making their own change in life. It's easy to tell somebody else to change, but try to convince yourself to change. It's one thing to say you're going to go to the gym and start losing weight. It's a completely different thing to say you're going to let your job or career go to start pursuing a dream. For some people, that's just not the right choice.

You have to be what I call a "blended optimist" to be a successful entrepreneur. You have to be willing to get back up off the ground after you've been totally destroyed. You need to be able to say, "You know what? I'm willing to try again, and there's going to be a success this time. If I try it this time, it's going to work." If you're a complete optimist and go through life with a carefree attitude, then owning a small business is a bad choice for you because you have peoples' lives at stake. You have whoever your investors are, you have your employees, you have your customers who are investing money into you, and if you're a total optimist who is just going to run down the road willy-nilly and think that everything's going to work out okay, then being an entrepreneur is not for you, because everything does not just work okay on its own.

The other part of being an entrepreneur is that you have to possess a willingness to take risks. You have to be *comfortable* taking risks. Risk is all relative to the individual. Some people think crossing the street outside of a crosswalk is a risk. Others will do crazy things like jump off of a mountain without hesitation. As an individual, you have to know your level of risk and your risk tolerance. To believe that you will be able to grow a business without taking risks, whether it's with your own personal money or your investors' money or a customer's money, is ridiculous. If you're not willing to make the decision to take some risks, you'll never progress.

Risk taking is a hard thing to do. Some people will make these decisions intellectually, but when it's time to actually pull the trigger in their business, which translates into their mortgage, which translates into their ability to put food on the table for their family, it becomes a different thing. I'm also not one who likes to hold up three-time entrepreneurs as good examples because they know what it means to fail. That's a cliché. "I like people who know what it means to fail." Really? Do you remember the last five teams that lost the Super Bowl? I understand that people fail, but this concept of needing to find people that like to fail? Those are people you *don't* want to work with.

What I mean by saying you need to be a blended optimist is that you have to be pessimistic at times. You have to have that inherent fear that something is going to go wrong, and you have to pay a lot of attention to detail. You have to overcompensate by working crazy hours to fix things that other people might not think need to be fixed.

Most entrepreneurs have a very high locus of self-control. As complicated as the world is, and as complex as the challenge of starting a business is, if you're not egotistical, you won't succeed. I'm not saying egotistical in a bad way. I'm not talking about the person with the big ego who thinks that they are better than everybody else. But at the end of the day you do have to believe that your idea is right, and you have to be willing to sacrifice whatever is needed, whether it's time or money, to be able to *prove* that your idea is right.

Without that initial belief in yourself, there is no way the business could ever start. You can be a manager or executive and not have that egotistical perspective, but to be an entrepreneur and create your own business you have to believe at your core that you have something special to offer.

To use a sports analogy, let's look at any team, say a basketball team. There's a whole team that plays basketball with five people on the floor, but there's always somebody on the team that they want to go to for the last shot to win the game when all the pressure is on. There are those players who are willing to do it because they're being asked and they're able to step up and focus themselves to do it. Then there are those who just want the ball—they want to be the ones to take the last shot. Those are two different types of players. And then there are the others who contribute by passing the ball to get it to you. Who's the entrepreneur in that group? Is it the guy that makes the final shot?

It could be the guy who's passing the ball to the guy who's making the shot. "Hey, I don't need to be taking the shot, but if you give me the ball, I'll get it to the player who's going to make the shot that's going to win the game for us." Sometimes the entrepreneur is the person who wants to take the last shot, but it doesn't necessarily mean that every single time it needs to be the player who wants to take the last shot. Sometimes it's the guy who's setting up the shot. Sometimes it's the player who's doing the pick-and-roll, or who understands the game better, or who knows who needs to take the shot or where the ball needs to go. So there is no hard and fast rule about being an entrepreneur.

You can teach the rules of the game. You can figure out who could be a success and who couldn't be. Some people are just naturally gifted at what they do. Some people, like me, had to work a lot of extra hours to make up for a lack of natural ability. I took a lot of lessons learned and spent a lot of time practicing and making mistakes and honing my craft to get where I am today. So while you can't teach somebody to be the player who's going to want the last shot or teach the person who wants to be the player with the ball to pass it to guy who has the last shot, you can teach them the game.

I am not a believer in hyping the player who took the last shot as the guy who won the game, because there were all those points before that got scored prior to the last shot, and there were all those points that *didn't* get scored by the other team because somebody else was playing defense. And there were all those people before who helped create the game. So for me, business is a *team sport*. It still takes key people in the organization to rally folks around and drive them to go forward. But you also have to be very introspective of yourself. That's when you truly become comfortable in your own skin and have the ability to be successful in business. You have to be able to look at yourself and decide if you're the guy who needs to have the ball, or do you just want to have the ball? Just because you want to have the ball and take the last shot doesn't mean you are the guy to do it.

The reality of being an entrepreneur is that you get to create your own rules. You get to create your own competition. If you don't like playing that game, you can change the game. You can go someplace else and play. You don't have to play against the big guy on the block. You can go down the street or to the next block over. You can even go to the next state over. You can do whatever you want to do.

If you want to be an entrepreneur, do it, but understand what you're doing. You have to *want* to do it, and you have to want to *learn*. At the end of the day you have to understand that once you become an entrepreneur, *you are not the company*. There are people like Steve Jobs that drove Apple to be successful, but Steve Jobs did not personally bend every piece of metal, solder every piece of circuit board to make the iPhone or iPod.

If you continue to push yourself to be the company and not let the company take precedence over you, the company is going to falter. It's a house of cards that can't continue to exist. You as the CEO embody the company's goals and visions and mission. Your job is to communicate and explain and help guide the company to success. People believe in you because you're personifying what the company is supposed to represent.

Successful CEOs stand for the goals of the company. They bring vision and ideas to the company and communicate them to the customers and the staff. That's their job. They successfully guide the company through the trials and tribulations of a business cycle.

When you're a start-up, entrepreneurs tend to overemphasize their own ability to contribute.

The second thing is that the employees aren't the CEO. You can't just clone yourself and think that they're going to replicate everything you say or make all the decisions you would make. As I said, you have to empower them and engage them in order for them to believe in what you're trying to do. Then you need to get them to agree to the ideals of where the company is supposed to go.

Again, it becomes an issue once the company and CEO become so linked and bound as one. Once that happens, the question is, if the CEO leaves will the company still survive? If not, then that would be the worst outcome: you build a company that's very successful, you check out, and the company completely fails because it was so dependent on you as an individual. Think about all those people you had working for you, all the employees who dedicated their careers to you because they believed in you. You raised the company up, and now you check out and the company goes down because you were so inextricably linked to the success of the business. That's not the outcome you want. It's not the outcome you worked so hard for.

You can't allow that to happen. The business is there to succeed, and the only way the business succeeds is when the customer is satisfied. The customer pays you, you then pay your employees, who go out and find the next customer and repeat the cycle. If you make yourself too much a part of that cycle and consume too much of it, eventually you won't have employees, nor will you have customers. Once it starts falling apart, you can't recover from it. Again, that's not the outcome you want.

What defines an entrepreneur? An entrepreneur is someone who risks money to make money. An entrepreneur is someone who is willing to work long, hard hours to bring his or her vision to fruition.

An entrepreneur is someone with guts. And the one thing I can promise you is that only on the street do you learn how to have guts.

TAKEAWAYS:

1. Starting up a business takes a lot of guts.

2. You have to be a "blended optimist" to be a successful entrepreneur.

3. If you're not willing to take some risks, you'll never progress.

TOP TEN LESSONS:

1. **It is all about you.** This is the greatest struggle of all. You must continuously strive to be self-aware enough to understand why you are taking on the challenges in life. Realize that there are no right and wrong choices . . . there is just your choice. Don't let someone else define that for you. At the end of the day, all you have is your belief in yourself.

2. **Your dream.** Take the time to dream without limitations. At one point in history, none of the ideas or concepts we used today were believed to be possible. By defining your ideal state, you can then set the tasks, conditions, and standards to start making active decisions to achieve your dreams.

3. **The ecosystem.** Everything has its own ecosystem, no matter how big or small. Whether it is your family, your job, a business, or an entire industry, they are relationships with inputs and outputs. Every ecosystem resists change. You need to be able to learn and adapt to survive.

4. **Reputation.** Your reputation is everything in business. You must continuously remain true to your values in everything you do. At the end of the day, customers and business partners work with you because of your reputation to deliver solutions to meet their needs. Don't ever lose sight of your reputation, and do all that you can to uphold it.

5. **Teamwork.** No one wins alone. There is always someone who helps along the way to set up the opportunity for success. Having the greatest team you can muster will always be the best way to win. I will always take a great

team with a mediocre plan over an average team with a great plan.

6. **Opportunity.** Opportunity surrounds you every day. It is in front of you all the time and everywhere. To maximize your chance for success, you need to constantly be aware of what is going on around you. Being aware of the ecosystem, of your team, and of all the impacts of external and internal events around you makes you better prepared to move when others are only looking.

7. **Risks.** Every decision in life has risks. Embrace the risk, and plan for it. Everyone has his or her own risk tolerance. If you are risk adverse, that is okay. Make your plans that way. Not everyone needs to swing for the fences every day.

8. **Courage.** We are only on this earth for a short time. You need to have the courage to try or even to say no. At the end of it all, the only thing you can take with you is that you had the courage to make the decisions you wanted to make. Do you really want to be left asking, "What if I had...?"

9. **Adapt or die.** Most things will not turn out like you had initially envisioned. You must have the ability to adapt to the things going on around you. Too often, the inability to adapt quickly is underemphasized. In order to be relevant, you must continuously look to adapt and improve in order to survive.

10. **Humility.** If you ever think you know it all . . . get out and fast. You are a danger to the business and everyone in it. Show up every day prepared to learn something new or how you can better yourself and the business. There is so much going on in the business world that you cannot know it all. Be a student of life and your own business to constantly do better every day.

TAKEAWAY SUMMARY:

1. Success is not about lessons learned in the classroom. It's about lessons learned on the street.

2. Three traits for a highly successful individual include perseverance, loyalty, and the courage to have a big idea.

3. Failure is not only an option—it is sometimes an inevitable outcome of decisions that you make.

4. Not trying is the biggest regret you will ever have.

5. Who are you? The more you can accept who you are and what you're trying to accomplish as part of your own vision and goals, the easier it will be to shape your future.

6. Clearly identify your idealized state—this will lead you to a better understanding of your sustainable business models.

7. Your reward may be the journey, so you have to want to be on this journey. If you're not able to get satisfaction from the relentless pursuit of the ideal state, you're going to miss out. There's not always going to be a pot of gold at the end of the rainbow, so you have to enjoy the adventure all the way through.

8. You must sell yourself. Networking is critical and powerful. Listen to your customers. Learn from your experiences. Connect with peers and potential customers.

9. Your brand must be transparent, and—just as important—it must be embedded within your organization's culture.

10. The market and the consumer are not merely data points. They are real people, real decision makers that require a certain level of human cultivation.

11. Incorporate situational awareness into your everyday practice. You have to understand what you want out of the business, what the business wants out of you, and where you're positioning the business to go.

12. Know your risk tolerance to effect change.

13. Visualize the outcome of the opportunity when it's presented to you. Process these thoughts, and make these decisions without going into analysis paralysis. The only way you can be truly confident that you will see an event window and know what to do is to practice it.

14. Understanding your role in your ecosystem and how you can best leverage the relationships that you foster within the ecosystem is crucial to a successful business.

15. Simply because you have a great product doesn't mean it will sell itself. You have to be able to understand the organizational level of how it's constructed, what it does, how it fits into the marketplace, and where the industry will allow it to go.

16. Don't get so caught up in the details that you miss an opportunity.

17. Listen. Understand. Actively engage.

18. What is your value proposition? Create and effectively deliver the message of your value proposition.

19. Human capital is the soul and the future of your organization. You must understand each individual's motivation for showing up to work every day and manage them so that they receive a return for their contribution.

20. You can't clone yourself! Take time to identify and groom the next generation in your company. Have the courage to empower and delegate staff to make decisions in the best interest of the organization.

David Morgan is cofounder and chief operating officer of STS International, where he oversees worldwide operations responsible for rapid design, development, and deployment of cutting-edge anti-terrorism and physical security technologies, medical simulation training applications, and professional engineering services. Through his innovations and strategic leadership, STS has achieved significant growth by penetrating new and emerging markets through a diversified client base in eighteen countries across four continents.

Morgan has led the development and deployment of programs to protect national interests for the Department of Defense, including the Department of the Army's biometrics program and the army's and the navy's intelligence, surveillance, and reconnaissance (ISR) technologies. He has deployed technical subject matter expertise to meet urgent Warfighter program requirements in Iraq, Afghanistan, and other austere locations. And he has led the development of medical simulation technologies for the army, air force, navy, and marines.

His strong commitment to research and development has translated his strategic vision into reality by producing technological and logistical advancements in the way in which US forces are supported in mission-critical operations. Advancements include: advance body armor solutions that were recognized in the Army Greatest Inventions program; command and control technology that consolidates full motion video (FMV) into common display systems; forming unique, highly skilled teams to provide sustainment operations, logistical support, and training to US forces throughout Iraq, Afghanistan, and other locations around the world for ISR and counter-improvised explosive device (C-IED) systems for the US forces deployed;

secure information screening, analysis, transfer, and dissemination in support of intelligence operations; and establishing the foundation and original program architectures for the development and integration of biometric technologies into DoD operations.

Morgan's core leadership principles are grounded in the strong belief that the investment in talented staff—and challenging the very best in his staff—is the greatest investment a company can make. Under his leadership, STS has grown almost 300 percent in the last three years. Most recently, STS was recognized as one of Inc.'s 5,000 Fastest Growing Companies in 2014 and 2015, and was a 2014 Small and Emerging Contractors Advisory Forum (SECAF) Government Project of the Year award finalist.

As a small business entrepreneur, Morgan has a true passion for mentoring young and emerging entrepreneurs. He served as a member of the board of directors of a nonprofit and currently as an advisory board member of several private companies. He is a regular speaker on innovation and entrepreneurship at the University of Maryland Smith School of Business and Georgetown University Law School. He is a member of the Dingman Center Angels, who evaluate and invest in premier start-up technology companies. Recognized for his leadership and evaluation of emerging technologies, David Morgan has been named to the National Institute of Justice Peer Review Panel and is an active reviewer of innovative approaches to analysis, research, and development; information and sensor technologies; investigative and forensic science and technology; and law enforcement technologies. He is a contributor to McGraw-Hill Publishers as a technical editor, reviewing training materials and publications for first responders and homeland security professionals in emergency operations and disaster response.

Based on his experiences, he has served as an advisor to many emerging professionals and over ten small businesses that span the defense and commercial industry. His community leadership and philanthropic efforts focus on service and include serving the community as a member of the Laurel Volunteer Rescue Squad and Prince George's County Fire Department for over two decades and supporting our nation's military through activities such as the Fisher House organization and Wounded Warrior programs.